The Future of International Economic Organizations

edited by
**Don Wallace, Jr.
Helga Escobar**

Published in cooperation with
the Institute for International
and Foreign Trade Law,
Georgetown University Law Center

The Praeger Special Studies program—
utilizing the most modern and efficient book
production techniques and a selective
worldwide distribution network—makes
available to the academic, government, and
business communities significant, timely
research in U.S. and international economic, social, and political development.

The Future of International Economic Organizations

PRAEGER SPECIAL STUDIES IN INTERNATIONAL BUSINESS, FINANCE, AND TRADE

Praeger Publishers   New York   London

Library of Congress Cataloging in Publication Data

Main entry under title:

The Future of international economic organizations.

(Praeger special studies in international business,
finance, and trade)
"Published in cooperation with the Institute for
International and Foreign Trade Law, Georgetown
University Law Center."
Papers presented at a colloquium held in Washington,
Oct. 31, 1975.
Includes index.
1. International economic relations—Congresses
2. International agencies—Congresses. I. Wallace,
Don, 1932–   II. Escobar, Helga. III. Georgetown
University, Washington, D.C. Institute for International
and Foreign Trade Law.
HF1411.F88   382.1'06   75-44942
ISBN 0-275-22990-4

PRAEGER PUBLISHERS
200 Park Avenue, New York, N.Y. 10017, U.S.A.

Published in the United States of America in 1977
by Praeger Publishers, Inc.

789 038 987654321

Printed in the United States of America

This book contains edited versions of papers and portions of the proceedings of a Colloquium on the Future of International Economic Organizations, cosponsored by the Institute for International and Foreign Trade Law and the Center for Strategic and International Studies of Georgetown University sponsored in Washington, D.C., on October 31, 1975. Two main themes ran through the colloquium: one related mostly to the United States and the other to international economic organizations.

The first theme was that America's self-confidence, damaged by its recent traumas, is not yet fully restored, its current concepts about the world and its role in it not yet fully clear, and the toughness of mind needed to deal with the world's economic problems somewhat lacking. The participants seemed agreed that this is not just a problem for Americans, and that the world will not move forward in international affairs as it should, unless there is effective and sustained leadership, and that this leadership must come from the United States.

The second theme, set out in Henry Costanzo's opening remarks, and confirmed by much of the subsequent proceedings, is the suggestion that there has been a possibly excessive proliferation of international economic organizations, even as the world's economic problems call for more leadership. There may be room for yet additional organizations, although Costanzo favored amendment of the old over creation of the new, room for improvement, and certainly room for coordination—but there is proliferation. Possibly this reflects a lack of lucid concept as to the nature and intensity of the underlying problems, possibly the limits of the present international political system. James P. Grant suggested that the demands of world economic problems simply had overloaded the present system. A general view was that some greater unification of efforts was in order. In my own view, the electric current, or motive force, moving through the machinery seems weaker than it should—again, possibly because of a lack of unified concept and leadership in the United States.

A related note at the colloquium was the disarray of U.S. government machinery to deal with international economic problems and organizations.

A third and possibly subsidiary theme was on differences in the underlying problems affecting the three areas—food, natural resources, and industrial trade—upon which effective international organizations are to be built. With respect to food, Edwin M. Martin suggested a lack of adequate data with respect to people's nutritional requirements. It is very hard to plan rationally in the field of agriculture when one does not know the market, that is, the demand for food. Similarly, it was suggested by Martin and others that agricultural policy remains peculiarly domestic in most nations, and not as susceptible to international leadership or negotiation as might be desired. With respect to natural resources, there was a good deal of discussion of the difficulties currently being encountered by private mining companies, investment by such companies apparently being important to the proper exploitation and marketing of these resources. With respect to industrial trade, a variety of problems was suggested ranging from the difficulty of negotiating improvements in nontariff barriers, again often more domestic in nature, through American leadership and congressional-executive relations problems, to the relationship of the General Agreement on Tariffs and Trade and the United Nations Conference on Trade and Development. It was suggested that UNCTAD should be preserved and its importance more appreciated in the United States.

The conclusion of the colloquium was the rather obvious one that international organizations would survive, but that they should be more rationally related, and that if this were done, more could be gained from them. This would be a gain to the United States, to the world, and to the prospects for an effective attack on the really large economic problems now facing the world.

I wish to thank my assistant, Helga Escobar, for her work in the editing of this book.

CONTENTS

LIST OF TABLES

LIST OF ABBREVIATIONS

ACC	Administration Committee on Coordination
AID	Agency for International Development
AIOEC	Association for Iron Ore Exporting Countries
CGFPI	Consultative Group on Food Production and Investment in Developing Countries
CGIAR	Consultative Group on International Agricultural Research
CIAP	Inter-American Committee on the Alliance for Progress
CIEC	Paris Conference on International Economic Cooperation
CIPEC	Inter-Governmental Council of Copper Exporting Countries
DAC	Development Assistance Committee
ECLA	Economic Commission for Latin America
ECOSOC	Economic and Social Council of the United Nations
GATT	General Agreement on Tariffs and Trade
GSP	Generalized system of preferences
IAEA	International Atomic Energy Agency
IBA	International Bauxite Association
IBRD	International Bank for Reconstruction and Development (now World Bank)
IFC	International Finance Corporation
IMF	International Monetary Fund
ITO	International Trade Organization
MFN	most favored nation
MTN	Multilateral Trade Negotiations
NATO	North Atlantic Treaty Organization
NIEO	New International Economic Order
NTB	Nontariff barrier
OAS	Organization of American States
OECD	Organization for Economic Cooperation and Development
OEEC	Organization for European Economic Cooperation (now OECD)
OEO	Office of Economic Opportunity
OPEC	Organization of Petroleum Exporting Countries
OPIC	Overseas Private Investment Corporation
PAG	Protein Advisory Group
SELA	Latin American System for Economic Cooperation
SITC	United Nations Standard International Trade Classification
UNCTAD	United Nations Conference on Trade and Development
UNCTC	United Nations Commission on Transnational Corporations

UNDP	United Nations Development Program
UNEP	United Nations Environmental Program
UNESCO	United Nations Educational, Scientific, and Cultural Organization
UNICEF	United Nations Children's Fund
UNIDO	United Nations Industrial Development Organization
USDA	United States Department of Agriculture
WFP	World Food Program
WHO	World Health Organization
World Bank	Formerly IBRD

1

THE COLLOQUIUM
Helga Escobar

The Colloquium on the Future of International Economic Organizations was held in Washington, D.C., on October 31, 1975. It consisted of three panel sessions in which the prospects for international organizations in the areas of food, natural resources (other than oil), and industrial trade were considered. A formally prepared paper for each panel was distributed prior to the meeting. It was summarized by the speakers at the meeting itself, and then discussed and evaluated by the commentators.

The colloquium sought to estimate the realistic outer limits of international organizations in the three specified areas, to delineate some of the characteristics of the international organizations that are likely to emerge, and to determine the significance they might have for American foreign policy.

What sorts of organizations can realistically be envisaged? How strong and effective can such organizations be? Would strong international institutions, if attainable, be helpful in the form in which they are likely to be attainable?

Finally, the colloquium addressed the question of whether an emphasis on international economic organizations or international organizations generally can contribute to a firm and well-oriented American foreign policy, especially in the area of economics.

CHAPTER

2

OPENING REMARKS
Henry Costanzo

It is a pleasure to initiate the discussions on the broad and timely topic of the role of international organizations in relation to three key elements in the world economy: food, nonoil natural resources, and industrial trade.

Both indirectly and directly, much of my career has been with international organizations in the financial field: the International Monetary Fund, the Inter-American Development Bank, and, since late last year, a Joint Ministerial Development Committee of the World Bank and the International Monetary Fund, which is itself an innovation on the international organizational scene. I recite this at the outset by way of confessing that my perceptions of the process of international cooperation through international organizations have been shaped in the special mold of these particular institutions.

I will not try to cover, even in summary fashion, the broad range of substantive issues that confront the international economic community today and that must be urgently dealt with—through international organizations or otherwise. For that purpose, Don Wallace has assembled a truly impressive array of distinguished individuals whose credentials and accumulated experience guarantee an exceptionally well-informed discussion. Instead, I would like to put forward a few general thoughts about international economic organizations, some of which most likely will hover in the background of the panel discussions and perhaps emerge as specific considerations in the round table that is to conclude the colloquium.

First, it must be acknowledged that this postwar period, representing most of our adult lives, has been historically unique in regard to international economic organizations. Indeed, the phenomenon of such organizations virtually dates from the end of

4

World War II, and international cooperation has become almost
synonymous with international organizations. More importantly,
the impulse to create new international machinery has been raised
to the level of a virtually automatic response on the part of national
government policy makers when new international problems arise.
I do not characterize this syndrome as good or bad, but simply note
that it does in fact exist.

Much of the international economic machinery created in the
last three decades falls into three main categories. There are the
specialized functional bodies created to carry out particular operational tasks, such as the international and regional banks for development lending, or the technical assistance agencies of the United
Nations, or the new agricultural fund being considered this week in
Rome. Then there are the consultative bodies for useful policy
exchanges, but usually without operational responsibilities, such
as the UN regional economic commissions; until recently in the
Western Hemisphere, the Inter-American Committee on the Alliance
for Progress; and the new Consultative Group on Food Production
and Investment in Developing Countries. Finally, there are the
bodies designed to mobilize the "political will" of governments
toward action in a particular problem area, or an area of effort,
with the implementation of any resulting agreed-upon initiatives
then entrusted to functional bodies of the first type. Examples that
come to mind of this third category are the UN Conference on Trade
and Development, the Development Assistance Committee, perhaps
the new energy producer-consumer conference of December 1975,
and certainly the Joint Ministerial Development Committee of the
World Bank and the International Monetary Fund.

I am not suggesting this three-way categorization as a definitive
analytic framework, but merely as a useful one. Certainly the
categories are not airtight, since some international bodies have
characteristics of more than one category. And perhaps another
category is needed to take account of a new phenomenon that might
be called the counterorganization, established not to forward a
perceived harmony among all nations but to defend or promote the
specialized interests of its limited membership, and reflecting the
simple fact that in international economic matters one should not
assume an exclusively altruistic interest in world cooperation to
be the only force motivating the establishment of organizations.

As far as the three main categories are concerned, it seems
that there may be some scope for further institution building of the
specialized functional type as new operational areas of international
concern emerge, possibly, for example, in relation to energy or
the exploitation of the seabed. But, broadly speaking, the obvious
fields of action in an operational sense appear already to be occupied

by competent bodies. Similarly, the scope for additional mechanisms of a general consultative nature appears limited, not least because the pace of international developments increasingly demands action and operationally oriented activities for which general consultative bodies are not well equipped.

Moreover, it is probably true that, with respect to these traditional forms of international organizations, we are rapidly reaching the point where the problems of proliferation may at least balance the benefits sought through new arrangements. Members of legislatures are not alone in having difficulty in keeping up with the "alphabet soup" on the international scene. Ministers of finance whom I personally observe in the Development Committee are becoming increasingly uncomfortable with the intricacies of the international organizational network.

It is not simply budgetary considerations that give rise to the concerns being expressed, nor an unreasoning desire to reach zero population growth in the considerable body of international civil servants. There are legitimate concerns that continued organizational growth without regard to the total pattern can in fact cause a dilution of effort, give rise to overlaps in responsibilities and conflicts in execution, and impose very serious burdens on governments in terms of the personnel and backstopping effort required for adequate representation and participation. Again drawing on personal experience, the converse of this from the side of international bodies is that the calendaring of international meetings is now a headache of the first magnitude, and often depends absolutely on the personal schedules of a few key and therefore overworked and overtraveled government representatives.

It seems, therefore, that the main effort in the period ahead might well be focused on the third general category. We need to consider how to adapt and make better use of international bodies that would be capable of mobilizing high-level government action. Umbrella organizations that can effectively coordinate and give coherent direction to the existing organizations in a given field of activity are needed. It makes little sense for the same governments in two different international bodies to promote lines of activity that are not mutually reinforcing or, in the worst case, perhaps are actually in conflict. And without institutions capable of taking an overview of the total international effort aimed at a given problem, how can appropriate international priorities be set and available resources rationally allocated?

Of course, part of the problem lies within participating governments themselves. When representation may be in the hands of the agriculture, commerce, energy, finance, or foreign ministry, depending on the international organization, there is the likelihood—

and I am afraid the likelihood may be great—that the same government
may reflect two different positions in two different organizations.
Only if both the international organizational structure and the support-
ing national hierarchies are able to integrate their respective
activities through what I would call overview organizations will
it be possible to raise the total productivity and improve the sense
of direction of the international system as a whole.

There is an important corollary to the point I have just made.
While I would not suggest there should be a moratorium on new
international organizations, I do think it is important to distinguish
between, on the one hand, the elaboration of new international tasks
and functions in response to emerging situations and, on the other,
the creation of new, independent international bodies to carry them
out. Given the broad array of existing institutions, in most cases
it would seem more appropriate to pour new wine into the service-
able bottles we have, rather than invest in new bottlemaking machinery
whose output remains to be tested. Where more is required than
simply assigning a new responsibility to an ongoing operation,
adaptation, even if by major surgery, seems preferable to the
creation of entirely new poles or centers of organizational activity
unrelated to what already exists.

The objective of all this, the achievement of which is an
important question underlying the forthcoming panel discussions,
is to meet the challenge of improving the system of international
intercourse through organizational means, not to tinker with one
part at the expense of another. This means, among other things,
that where components of the system evolved historically in a way
that omitted participation by important elements in the world
economy, such as, for example, the nations of Eastern Europe or
the newly important oil-producing countries, adaptation in a correc-
tive sense is desirable. In addition to promoting universality, we
need to weigh every new organizational proposal in terms of its
contribution to a rational division of labor. Our emphasis now
should be on integration, not expansion.

Since we are dealing specifically with international economic
organizations, I do not think we can avoid facing the issue of how
differences in the relative economic power of the participants
should be reflected in the structure and functioning of such organizations. Every international forum for dealing with economic problems
is a testing ground where the strong will seek to employ their
strength to advantage and the weak will seek to offset their weakness
and improve their position. This is, after all, what the so-called
new international economic order is all about, and is relevant to
the various proposals made for restructuring the economic activities
of the United Nations.

There is, undoubtedly, greater recognition today by the world's wealthy countries that the situation of the poor countries cannot continue without giving rise to instability damaging to their own interests. But are the wealthy countries prepared to entrust the process of ameliorating the situation of the poor to organizations structured on the political, rather than economic, principle of General-Assembly-style democracy? If not, how far are the wealthy prepared to go in recognizing the aspirations of the poor, and how far are the poor prepared to go in recognizing the economic preponderance of the wealthy?

No proposals that fail to come to grips with this issue will prove to be realistic and viable ones. I am sure our panelists are sensitive to it, and I look forward, as I am sure you all do, to their analyses and their prescriptions on how international organizations could best help in meeting the massive problems in the world economy.

Finally, I should like to congratulate the sponsors of this colloquium for having selected and called to our attention a subject that is very timely indeed and that certainly represents a key aspect of problems facing us.

PROSPECTS FOR INTERNATIONAL ORGANIZATIONS IN THE AREA OF FOOD

3

INTERNATIONAL INSTITUTIONS IN THE FOOD FIELD
Edwin M. Martin

It may seem a little strange to devote a panel to defects in the international institutional system dealing with the world food problem just one year after the World Food Conference covered the subject rather comprehensively in its Resolution XXII. Such treatment can only be justified on two grounds: that its resolution contained errors or gaps or that its proposals have not been, or at least not properly, implemented.

In evaluating the current prospects, arrangements to deal with several questions broader than the food problem must be taken into account. Clearly, satisfactory progress in seeing that everyone gets an adequate diet depends on proper actions at several levels, as well as on several closely related but different subjects.

Internationally adequate trading, monetary, and financial institutions and systems are required because an adequate volume of food production is dependent on an effective world system for supplying physical, financial, and technical inputs and for purchasing surplus outputs. Proper distribution of foods to those who need it depends on a global transport and marketing network, especially given the growing dependence of developing countries on imports of basic grains.

In addition to sound international economic policies and priorities of the general sort referred to, the food system, for the foreseeable future, is heavily dependent on orderly world arrangements for maintaining adequate supplies at reasonable prices of energy from nonrenewable sources. Partially affecting this but also having a direct impact on food supplies is the need for efficient long-term management in the global interests of the resources of the sea and the seabed.

To an extent not always recognized, the food task is reduced by global progress in more general health measures, such as educating some people to eat less meat and meat products and eliminating many more of the parasites and persistent infections that can consume a disturbingly large portion of the afflicteds' daily intake. This program also has, of course, its international institutional leadership.

Last, but not least, the magnitude of the food task is directly conditioned on the rate of population growth, a subject that is increasingly accepted as a not just proper but necessary subject for international policies and institutions.

What I conclude from this listing is not that one can find many alibis for failure of international food agencies alone to making more progress in solving our food problems, but the need to be aware of the necessity for ensuring an integrated and interdependent attack on them through close institutional links, constitutionally and in daily practice, between the responsible international authorities in these various sectors, each operating under the at least general policy guidance of an all-embracing global politicoeconomic institution. Nor is this emphasis on having a well-organized set of international policies and institutions intended to convey the impression that they can see that everyone is fed. As Secretary of Agriculture Earl L. Butz has often said, "only farmers grow wheat." In some ways even more significant is the fact that only correct national policies can give farmers the incentives and means to do so.

In my subsequent suggestions, I do not challenge the effective sovereignty of the nation-state. It can be, and is being, infringed upon in a number of fields. However, I do not think that the nature of national food production and distribution systems, or of the economic structures that affect so directly the ability of some people to be well nourished and others not, permits, let alone encourages, such infringements. We can provide internationally valuable economic and technical information that no nation can produce alone and that will usually have an affect on policies and actions. UN conferences can recommend a long series of actions that would be in the global interest for every government to take, and do so unanimously, without any government taking the decision to act accordingly. We are still in an era of international persuasion, coaxing, and finger-pointing, but no more. Even international financial institutions face limits to the steps they can bribe governments to take by offering loans if they do and none if they do not.

With this introduction, what about international organizations in the food field? We now have a long list of them at our disposal.

The new World Food Council at the political level, elected by and under the UN General Assembly though reporting to it through the Economic and Social Council (ECOSOC), is at the top. Its establishment, in the face of the existence of FAO, derived from at least four factors:

1. FAO was one among a number of members of the UN family with some responsibilities related to the food system, such as WHO, WMO, UNIDO, UNICEF, UNDP, PAG, the World Bank, and WFP, and could not coordinate the work of the others.
2. There was dissatisfaction with the effectiveness of FAO, partly as a bureaucratic institution and partly because of the low level of participation in its council meetings and the burden on it of budget and other details that prevented the council from dealing with broader issues.
3. Some thought that, over the years, FAO had become in some ways country oriented and conservative.
4. FAO was not fully representative as the USSR, of growing importance in the food field, refused to join.

While these points have varying degrees of merit, I think they were probably overshadowed by the unspoken belief that FAO had cried wolf for so many years and gotten so tied up in people's minds with the existing order of things that it was no longer listened to and a new voice was required to arouse public opinion.

It is too early to pass judgment on what improvements the World Food Council will be able to bring about, but on paper it fills the need for strategic leadership.

Directly under the World Food Council were proposed two committees, one on food security and one on food aid. The constitution of the former depends on ratification of the Agreement on World Food Security, under discussion in the FAO for two years and endorsed by the World Food Conference. Its task would be to oversee the implementation of the agreement, a broad document covering a good many fields now dealt with by FAO. A new role for the committee depends probably on what steps are taken to establish food reserves. It might stimulate follow-up on the relevant provisions of the agreement, probably in close cooperation with FAO. It might also receive reports from, and oversee the activities of, whatever organization may be established by the major grain exporters and importers who were asked by the World Food Conference to meet as soon as possible to "accelerate" the implementation of the provisions of the agreement by organizing an international system of national grain reserves. This negotiation is still in process with disagreement as to whether it should take place primarily under the auspices of the International Wheat Council or in GATT (General Agreement on Tariffs and Trade) trade negotiations.

While institutional arrangements of a modest sort will be required to operate any agreement that may be set up, the present situation suggests that it may not be easy to work out their nature and locus. Probably a committee with a small staff, perhaps supported administratively by the able Secretariat of the International Wheat Council, will be required, operating independently but reporting on its activities to the World Food Council through the Committee on Food Security, but not taking orders from either of them. This may prove to be the most workable arrangement. Recommendation on when to buy and when to sell can hardly be reached wisely by public international voting procedures in which many participants are not mainly involved in the effects of the decision taken or able to be well informed on what are highly complicated and technical matters that must be worked out in private discussions.

If action is put in the hands of the major participants in the grain trade, it will be given to countries who are exporters and importers, rich and poor, with market and centrally planned economies.

The Committee on Food Aid is well on its way to being formed by a reconstitution of the Intergovernmental Working Group, half chosen by the FAO Conference and half by the General Assembly, which supervises the World Food Program.

It must deal with a number of policy issues regarding the handling of food aid. It is debatable whether these should include indications of volumes needed annually by individual countries since such estimates would require these countries to make available for commercial food inputs data not only on the size of food deficits but also on the foreign exchange resources.

Assuming it can get adequate staff advice to perform this function from FAO, the International Monetary Fund (IMF), the World Bank, or the World Food Council Secretariat, there remains the task of securing pledges to finance the import of this amount of food. A burden-sharing exercise of this sort can only be performed privately in discussions among the few countries with the capability of acting, not in a public meeting with more potential recipients than donors participating. Often bilateral exchanges or quiet individual contacts between a senior international official and the potential donors must be the first step. Decisions may be made public at meetings of the Committee on Food Aid or the World Food Council, but neither is an appropriate negotiating forum. This may be one useful lesson from the not wholly successful first meeting of the World Food Council.

Some may propose a formal donor's group in which pledging and follow-up on pledges would take place, as has been done by the

committee responsible for the implementation of the Food Aid
Convention. I am not sure that formalizing the list of potential
donors by having them on a committee would be useful at this time
in view of the present uncertainties about who should be and who is
willing to be included, having in mind not only OPEC (Organization of
Petroleum Exporting Countries) but also those with centrally planned
economies. Later, perhaps, this could be done with a loose connection made to the Committee on Food Aid and through it to the World
Food Council.

With respect to investment in food production in developing
countries, a top priority in the view of the World Food Conference,
the World Bank, FAO, and the UN Development Program were asked
by that meeting to establish a Consultative Group on Food Production
and Investment in Developing Countries (CGFPI) to increase the flow
of investment, better coordinate it, and improve its efficiency. It
is a rather informal and flexible body composed of old and new,
bilateral and multilateral, donors who in their view have an interest
in the subject; two countries from each of the five FAO regions
chosen by the countries of the region; and representatives of any
other body the chairman thinks can contribute to the discussion of
a particular agenda item.

CGFPI does not vote or have money to spend, operating by
persuasion and exchange of information and experience. Its first
two meetings were held in July 1975 and February 1976. It will be
some time before the degree of its influence on actions can be judged.

With the hope of attracting additional funds, especially from
new donors concerned about the food problem and interested in an
institution whose policies they could control better than they can
those of existing ones, the World Food Conference proposed the
establishment of an International Fund for Agricultural Development.
It would collect funds and set policies for their expenditure, but
turn over the actual handling of projects to the staffs of the World
Bank and the three regional banks.

This organization will not come into being until the UN Secretary-
General determines that enough money has been pledged to justify
establishing a new bureaucracy. With the endorsement of a U.S.
contribution of $200 million toward an initial target of $1 billion,
announced in the speech of Secretary of State Henry Kissinger to
the UN Special Session, the prospects for the fund look good,
although several congressional hurdles still have to be jumped.
Without the United States, its prospects are dim. It is expected
that it would, like other international institutions financing investments in food production, be a participant in CGFPI.

The important resolution of the World Food Conference on research was turned over to the already proven Consultative Group on International Agricultural Research (CGIAR). Insofar as progress can best be made through international centers, working on reasonably early payoff projects, its record is excellent. However, there is a gap in the international machinery at two ends. Due to constraints of funds, and partly perhaps of people, CGIAR and its technical advisers on its Technical Advisory Committee have been reluctant to sponsor really basic research or the exploration of radical ideas with only modest chances of practical use in the next decade or so, if ever.

In our first major effort in research on basic tropical food crops, we need to seek prompt results, as CGIAR has done. But as population keeps growing and fossil-fuel energy keeps costing more and more, we also need to be better prepared for the pressures of 2000 and beyond on food supplies in the tropics. Preferably, the donors of CGIAR should insist on funding a more adventurous research effort in addition to the present essential applied one.

At the other end, the CGIAR program has done much to transmit its results to national institutions, to help them by training at the centers, by assigning professional advisers, and by exchanging publications and plant materials to further the essential adaptation to local requirements of the new seeds and cultural practices they have produced. But this help has not been enough, and many of the national research establishments remain underfinanced, understaffed, and not closely linked to national priorities or well informed about farmers' problems.

While the International Center System is aware of what needs changing, it is naturally fearful that acceptance of a continuing responsibility for encouraging and coordinating more help from bilateral and multilateral donors to these essential transmission belts will weaken its ability to perform its central and certainly very high priority task. As an alternative, it has been suggested that CGFPI may be the logical body to deal with the coordinated investment of money and people required to build up the role and competence of national research institutions as essential components of national food systems. The matter is now pending between the two bodies with a resolution hoped at the end of 1976, neither anxious to infringe on the proper role of the other. It is a thorny problem, with the delicate task of research management at the heart of many of the failures, and reluctance to take it on is understandable.

Nutrition is another vital field for which adequate institutional coverage has not yet been organized at the international level. Dealing with it wisely and vigorously is basic. The whole food system must be judged in the end by the level of nutrition it provides. The choices made by consumers to fill what they see to be their nutritional priorities provide the signals to the whole food production effort. Both FAO and WHO are deeply involved in nutrition, but much more deeply in other matters. UNICEF has been properly active on this subject since protein deficiencies in the diets of very young children have irreversible effects on mental and physical capacities. But it, too, has many other concerns. The World Food Program acts to improve nutrition, but by the limited tool of food aid projects. The only UN body solely concerned with nutrition is the Protein Advisory Group, but it is largely technical and research rather than program oriented.

The World Food Conference recognized the weakness of this dispersion of responsibility and asked ECOSOC to consider the need for an effective coordinating mechanism. It has not yet done so pending the completion of studies of the problem in a working party of the Administration Committee on Coordination (ACC), an internal UN body on which all the components of the UN system sit and try to coordinate their activities. It is to be feared that they may avoid tackling the clash of jurisdictions or the gaps to be filled head-on, but settle for another committee of agency heads to meet once or twice a year to negotiate on clashes around the edges. Far more than this is needed.

All the agencies mentioned have a role that bears on nutrition, but leadership that will focus them on a common major effort is lacking. It is especially critical as national governments in developing countries are even less aware of the need for special efforts and are almost wholly unequipped now with the personnel to mount major drives on this front, badly needed as they are. The object is partly humanitarian, but it is also an investment in productive capacity and a major potential saving in the cost of education and medical care and in investments in food production. Eating the right things, properly prepared, can decrease materially the present unacceptable levels of waste between the farmer's field and the consumer's health.

Vital food production inputs are fertilizer and a wide range of pesticides, herbicides, and so on. Work in this area is largely focused in FAO, with close, well-established cooperation among it, UNIDO, the World Bank, CGFPI, and the industries involved. Nothing more seems needed, although the various organizations have many problems to solve.

A considerable list of more technical subjects related to the global food system is handled with a usually high level of technical competence in FAO. One special matter on which the World Food Conference urged a new effort is that of a Global Food Information and Early Warning System. FAO has moved to expand its already considerable work in this field. The main problems are the failure of two major grain producers and consumers—the USSR and the People's Republic of China—to cooperate thus far and the lack of good data about food production in a long list of countries, some of them important.

I have not mentioned coordination of national agricultural policies. Undoubtedly the world is highly interdependent, and decisions to take land out of production in the United States or to increase the cattle population of the USSR by imports regardless of domestic crop output affect everyone's food budget. But I see no role for a new international organizational attack on these politically sensitive decisions, intimately tied to domestic political influences as they are, regardless of formal systems of government. For what the international community can do, the World Food Council and FAO can and are trying to provide the required leadership.

4

INTRODUCTION
Edwin M. Martin

My rather brief paper described the present organizational situation in the food field—a rather considerable number of bodies, mostly within the UN system, that have this exclusive responsibility. There are, of course, others that deal with it in part. I have tried to set forth where I thought things stood in terms of adequacy of the present setup.

I will not repeat that essentially descriptive and only briefly analytic document, but there are several general points I would like to make. Partly this is to catch the other members of the panel without time to prepare to comment on these remarks, maybe engendering more impromptu replies.

First, I think that success in dealing with the food problem depends on the success of other international organizations in other fields. Whether it is through trade arrangements, financial arrangements, family planning programs, or even law of the sea, to say nothing of the energy problem, food success is not easy, if at all possible, without a reasonable degree of effective world organization and activity in these other fields. They do not guarantee success, but they are a very important condition of it.

Second, the food organizations operate with an absence of information where it is most important, namely, in the poorer parts of the world, in the developing countries, and this is because the nature of the economic sector is unique. There is no other sector that has several hundred million independent entrepreneurs. Collecting

information on their activities has proved thus far well beyond the
capacity of the statistical structures. I might even say that so far
we have been totally unable to find out how much developing country
governments are investing in food production, which is a relatively
simple piece of information, as compared with what farmers are
investing. Therefore, we operate with a very minimum of basic
data in terms of planning or judging success.

Third, one cannot overemphasize the degree to which international arrangements or planning or decision making with respect
to food impinge on domestic policy issues of a high political character.
One talks about a major trend in international affairs, particularly
international economic affairs, being the increasing mix with domestic
policy issues, and the difficulty of separating the two. Well, there
is no area where this is more acute than in the case of food.

Now, as a result, as a fourth point, I think you will find that
the considerable number of food organizations are all very much of
a consultative character, a recommendatory character—they have
nothing corresponding to even the authority with which the International Monetary Fund (IMF), for example, is entrusted—just
because no country, developed or developing, is willing to cede any
considerable degree of control or authority or even very precise
direction without authority to an international organization. I do not
think this can persist; we have to move beyond this. How we will do
so is hard to say. There have been suggestions of something like an
IMF type of organization that would negotiate standby agreements
in which help is offered for food production in return for the recipient
doing A, B, or C in terms of food policy. I doubt if this is operable
at the present time.

But I suspect the first area in which we should be moving into
a sanction type of operation is in the handling of an international
system of food reserves. It has been the U.S. proposal that people
who play the game will get preferential access to food when they
need it. But so far, it hasn't been bought by others in very concrete
terms. This reserve negotiation is one of the most important and
still one of the most difficult and unpromising in the food area.

On the other hand, insofar as recommendations and nonmanda-
tory types of activity are concerned, there is a common recognition
of the importance of the food issue and a substantially involved
bureaucracy in most countries. As a result, we have managed thus
far to avoid most of the political confrontation atmosphere that has
dogged some of the other sectors. Despite a great deal of oratory,
I think the food conference was notable for the degree to which,
when we got down to the specifics of resolutions dealing with the
food problem, the debate was on substance and not on politics, the
substance of what is the best thing to do.

I hope this can be continued, but it will not be easy, especially as there is still one gap, an important one, namely, that two of the great food producers and consumers with enormous impacts on world trade and basic staples—the Soviet Union and the People's Republic of China—are not active participants in most of this debate. The Soviets have refused to join FAO. When I chided them once last year that the alleged reason that it cost too much—$4 or $5 million a year—was nonsense for the great Soviet Union, I was chided back with "ah, yes, but we make our expenditures on the basis of cost-benefit ratios." Although the Chinese are members, they are not participants in any real sense. Thus, we are operating without any real contributions from them or a real capability of having an impact of any sort, through persuasion or otherwise, on these two great powers. This is an important limiting factor.

Finally, I would like to stress that the objective of a food system is to feed people better, particularly the people that are not getting enough of the right foods to eat, those malnourished 400 or 500 million. Yet, as in so many other areas of economic activity, particularly among the industrialized countries, the emphasis in public debate and private action tends to be almost exclusively on the production of food, and not on its consumption.

Nutrition is the empty chair at the table, and almost no governments have nutrition plans or nutrition expertise in their planning organizations. Most international financial institutions do not have a nutrition expert on their staffs. Or, in the case of the biggest, there is only one real expert on the staff out of 4,000 employees. As yet, we know relatively little about nutrition. But we do even less with what we know. There are enormous opportunities to reduce the burden on scarce resources in food production and to decrease malnutrition, if we would just pay some serious attention to nutrition as such. This is not just a question of developing countries, although they have the most serious problems and are doing the least about it at a government level, but also of developed countries.

The degree of quackery that envelopes the field of diet and nutrition is almost beyond belief, when eating has such a central role to play in how well we can perform, how well we can enjoy our life and our quality of life. Unfortunately, we have no central institution any place in the international system focusing with any degree of authority on the nutrition issue. It's divided up in quarreling entities at the present time.

Our first commentator is John Schnittker. He is one of those rare people who has combined a successful career as a professor and a high government official—I should not say bureaucrat as he was undersecretary of agriculture, which is a strictly political job—

and now is meeting a payroll, all involved in the problems of food and agriculture. Our second panelist is James P. Grant, president of the Overseas Development Council. He has just returned from China, where he was born. Of course, he has been a good many places, and his travels have given him as broad a contact as anybody, I think, in this country with the problems of development, of which food, in whose production some 70 to 75 percent of the population of developing countries are involved, has a central role.

COMMENT
John Schnittker

I accepted this assignment somewhat reluctantly, partly because meeting the payroll takes me so far away from the specific area that we are talking about today, that I seriously wonder whether I have anything to say. But I will make a few comments, and depend upon James Grant and your questions to draw out the main points of the discussion.

I'm glad that Edwin Martin took a very modest view of the role of international organizations in world agricultural affairs, world agricultural development, food reserves, or whatever other issues may come up. In my opinion, one can hardly take too modest a view of the role of international organizations, either in the past ten or twenty years or in the next ten years in world agricultural and food matters.

I'm not prepared to say that one should disband FAO and other organizations that are concerned with food. I do think that we probably should keep working toward some very big objectives, such as the establishment of some kind of international coordinating agency with the capability of sanctions along the lines of IMF. However, I am extremely pessimistic about the 20- or 30-year achievements of such an objective. In some of the debating societies of the agricultural sector, like the International Wheat Council and the International Sugar Organization, it has been worthwhile to continue the organization, and to keep talking, even after whatever teeth had once been in a wheat agreement or a sugar agreement had been pulled. But we should not expect very large or very quick results, nor should we be disappointed with failure to achieve results.

In getting to Edwin Martin's paper, in contrast to his introduction to these comments, I want to mention one or two specific points. First, he mentions that we can justify this colloquium possibly only on one of two grounds: that the resolutions of the World Food Conference contained errors or gaps or that its proposals have not been, or at least not properly, implemented. On the first point,

I don't know whether or not there were errors or gaps—I have never read it. On the question of implementation, it seems to me much too early to expect implementation of a conference that took place only a year ago. If there is a serious problem, it is a much more fundamental one in expecting too much from quasi-events like the World Food Conference, and therefore having disappointments arise from unrealistic hopes.

A second point in Martin's paper (and a trivial one, actually) is his expression of hope of progress in such matters as, "educating some people to eat less meat." My own view is that this is worse than hopeless. One may, by virtue of circumstances, force people to eat less meat, either by political rationing or by economic rationing through a price system. Otherwise, I view the efforts of the past year to plead with people to eat less meat as quite useless.

The demand for meat in the world is a homogeneous function of the level of disposable income, and when Chinese, Russians, Burmese, Indians, Europeans, and Americans get more income, they are going to want more meat. Perhaps they won't be able to get it, but they want it.

What about specific organizations in the food area? Martin notes that FAO, on the record at least the principal organization in the world relating to food and agricultural matters, was bypassed by the World Food Conference in setting up implementation of projects and programs of the World Food Conference. Given the state of FAO these past ten years or so, I suspect that this was probably the right thing to do. I'm not sure that setting up new organizations was the right thing to do. The world will have to face up to the problem one of these days of shaking up the international organizations, strewing the bureaucracy of FAO on the Roman landscape via budget cuts or via some other crisis, before one can really get a unit like that to function.

There is an issue arising next month, the selection of a new director-general for FAO. I have not followed it in detail, but I assume that the selection of a director-general has a lot to do with what the world expects FAO to do the next five years. Based upon experience in that selection five years ago, I would not have high hopes for the process.

Other international organizations, while certainly useful, and probably having a high cost-benefit ratio, have also the potential for doing a lot of damage. I refer even to such august and honored bodies as the World Bank. I have been in a few developing countries where agricultural development is looked upon as a few World Bank projects. One asks, "What is your policy with respect to the development of beef production?" They respond, "We have one or two World Bank projects." When you look at them, these projects have almost no relationship to the possibilities for the development of a beef industry. They may be pilots or models, but they do not represent the rising tide that will lift all the boats. They simply are too small, but they become the showcase that often becomes the rationale for not doing something sensible to develop all of the resources of a country capable of development.

Martin mentioned the problems of domestic policies. Most countries of the world have domestic agricultural policies that are politically sacrosanct. Back in the early 1960s, in connection with the Kennedy Round trade negotiations, someone coined the term—an objective—that in the Kennedy Round, we should deal not just with quotas and tariffs but with national agricultural policies. This became the great agricultural platitude of the Kennedy Round. We kept saying it because it had been said in so many high places, but we couldn't do it. I continue to believe that this is an objective worth maintaining. We can build a few stepping-stones toward the achievement of that objective, but it is essentially unreachable.

Finally, a word on the food reserves issue. There is an international organization currently considering the procedures for establishment of an international food reserve. The United States has made a proposal for a 25 million ton reserve of wheat, supplemented by 5 million tons of rice, as a start in this area. I support this, and I hope that it succeeds in the next few years, but I want to give you my scenario for success in this area.

Most of the major countries taking part in this project are not serious about it. I say this particularly about the United States. The people from the Agriculture Department who represent us in those meetings devote their time principally to avoiding the establishment of a world food reserve. But apart from that, I see only a series of good crops in the world establishing, creating a visible surplus that we can then call a reserve, as the circumstances that will force the world to look at the rules for handling the reserve.

Many of us thought we had a chance this past summer, but it was headed off by bad weather in July. Perhaps next year. Finally, I would say on reserve, as long as we have a very narrow balance between the supply of grains, which are the principal foodstuffs of the world, and the demand at about current prices, we are not going to make progress in international reserve discussions or in organizations that carry out an international reserve program.

COMMENT
James P. Grant

There are three points in regard to Edwin Martin's paper that I want to underline. The first is the galaxy of the institutions described in the food field, and this brings one head-on to the kind of issue that John Schnittker raised: Were new institutions required or could one have just reformed the existing FAO structure? My own reply to that, in short, is no. I will come back to that later.

Second, I want to underline Martin's comment that success in the world food front depends very heavily on progress in other fields, requiring major changes. He mentioned energy and health, which led to the question of eating styles—maybe not for all the reasons that Martin originally indicated, but for a package of reasons.

Third, he mentions that the resolutions of the World Food Conference were really only the starting point, that to get a UN resolution did not mean necessarily that anything would happen. I think this needs to be underlined strongly, as we now go into not only continued implementation of the World Food Conference's resolutions but of all the concepts that have come out of the Seventh Special Session.

I think that this particular meeting is very timely, and that one can safely make the statement that the world in the next 18 months faces the prospect of more negotiations on more issues in more forums on matters that vitally affect the well-being of human beings than ever before in the history of the world. And I do not think that there is any gearing up yet, really, to face up to this multiplicity of issues, negotiations, forums, and the like. This is particularly significant, because it is quite clear to me that what progress has been made since November 1974 in implementing the World Food Conference's resolutions has been due in significant part, as far as the United States is concerned, to private and congressional pressure on the administration to follow through on some general points. If this same set of factors is to apply, it does mean that the private sector has got a major organizational sorting out job to do if it is to play its important role with Congress and the executive branch.

It is quite clear that the galaxy of proposals coming out of the World Food Conference and the Seventh Special Session cannot be implemented unless there is a fairly strong global will to do so. This immediately raises a most fundamental point that this colloquium needs to consider: Is the world faced with a situation where we are just tinkering with a series of structures, or are we faced with a situation where we really need to hammer out a new global economic order for a wide variety of reasons, of which the demand of the developing countries for a new international economic order is just a facet?

Do we regard the demands of the developing countries for a new international economic order as just a group of one-way demands? Whatever they get is going to be something less for us. Or do we have the kind of requirement for a new order that, if we can integrate their requirements into our new requirements, we can come up with a mixture of new structures and mechanisms—similar, it seems to me, to what was done between 1945 and 1950 with the Bretton Woods and the United Nations.

I would say that the corporate response of the administration to date, certainly prior to the Seventh Special Session, was that the world really requires only tinkering, and that as you deal with the demands of the developing countries for a new international economic order, we were in a winners and losers context. Therefore, I do think it is important to underline briefly the reasons why we are in a situation that requires a new global economic order that will meet our needs.

The current crises in the world obviously are due in part to short-term cyclical factors with which we are all familiar: the droughts around the world, the boom, the Middle East war. I think we are faced with a set of circumstances that Lincoln Gordon touches on in his paper. We face a whole set of discontinuities in the supply and demand in global systems. I would argue that the world faces a systems overload on such a myriad of fronts that the whole world faces this situation. The world went from a $1 trillion gross global product in 1949-50 to a $3 trillion gross global product in the early 1970s in constant dollars, and we began to find the demands of growth outrunning the response capacity of global institutions.

I join Gordon in taking rather sharp exception to many of the findings of the Club of Rome. But I would underline his point that what we do face is a major adaptive problem, and as we went into that third trillion dollars of gross global product in the late 1960s, we began to see first all our problems of environmental overload: pollution of the cities, the eutrophication of lakes, the multiyear decline of the world fish catch from overharvesting. We have begun to go into circumstances where, because of growing demand, raw material areas that historically had been buyer's markets shifted to seller's markets, the most graphic illustration of which is the oil field. As one shifted to a buyer's market, power was shifted to a group of people who had been out of the power system before. Because the political side of the system had not taken care of their needs, there was a systems breakdown in the energy area.

We saw in certain fields, such as food and fertilizer, a multi-year shortage occurring and we found the circumstance of the 3 percent shift in supply leading to a 250 percent increase in price in the world food situation. The world's most fundamental demand and a major breakdown in that system occurred. We began to worry about the environmental concerns this meant for the United States, and we slowed down the development of new oil in Alaska. At the same time, the environmental concerns increased our con-

sumption of fuel through the requirements on autos, so we got less
and less mileage. And just as our own supply decreased and our
demand went up, we got thrown into a global demand burden on the
Middle East at a time when they were demanding additional goods,
additional quid pro quos out of the system.

It is quite clear that if the world is to continue the growth rate
of the period from the early 1960s to the early 1970s, on the basis
of 1950 dollars, the gross global product of the world would go from
something like $3 trillion to somewhere between $10.5 and $12
trillion by the end of the century.

If we have encountered these problems of adaptation, as we
went from that second to the third trillion, what would happen if
we were to reach that tenth or eleventh trillion by the end of the
century? I suggest that, first, the world is not going to reach
twelve trillion by the end of the century and, second, whether or
not we drastically fall short of that at a level of 6, 7, or 8 trillion,
instead of 9 or 10 trillion, depends largely upon whether or not we
can hammer out a set of new institutional structures to adapt to
these problems in the food, energy, and trade fields.

That is the central challenge we face. How do we avoid a
permanent massive reduction in global growth? How do we get it
going again? If we assume that even when we get it going again,
it will be somewhat slower, how do we handle the distribution
problems both within the rich countries and globally?

The second major factor that needs to be taken into account as
part of this new institution-building mix is that there are two
problems of growth without adequate sharing that need to be factored
in. The first is the problem of growth without adequate sharing
between countries. Essentially, in its broadest sense, this is a
sort of historic shift that we have seen since about 150 years ago
when the disparity between the richest countries and the poorest
countries (the richest 10 percent of the world and the poorest
10 percent of the world) was maybe two or three to one. Today,
in dollar terms, it is fifty to one. Probably, in real terms, if you
consider the upper 10 percent of the world and the poorest 10 percent
of the world, it may be 15 times the ratio of disparity. It's getting
worse, and it is this factor that has led to a series of demands that
need to be factored in.

There has been the sort of circumstances we recognized initially
in UNCTAD. Then, most recently, it has come to the fore in the
demands for a new international economic order. Somehow these
demands need to be taken into account in the new institution building.
Second, out of the crises of the last two or three years, a new
phenomenon has emerged, basically a fourth world where the growth
is likely to be significantly slower for those countries over the next

15 years than for the last 15 years unless something very special is done in the institutional structures of the world. Finally, we have the problem that some of the developing countries are beginning to gain enough power so that, unless we pull them into the system, they promise to have the capacity to disrupt the world systems as the Germans did pre-World War I and the Germans and the Japanese did pre-World War II. We do need to figure out a way to allow the Brazilians, the Mexicans, and the more powerful OPEC members to play a major role in the new institutions. Otherwise, somewhere along the line the system's going to crack from too slow a response.

The second half of the growth-without-adequate-sharing problem occurs within the developing countries. Most of them face a situation where the income disparities within countries are considerably more acute than they were within the West when the developed countries went through comparable periods of growth. This raises a series of additional problems that need to be taken into account.

First, we see a circumstance where one major society in the world has met this problem: the Chinese. This is going to have a profound political impact globally over the next 20 years unless something comparable can be done for the poorer developing countries in the market economy side of the world. Second, as the developing countries in the global forums push the developed countries to make concessions, in part through power but in part through the argument of equity, the reply to the developing countries will be, "We will do this on equity grounds if we have some assurance that this will beneficially affect all those within your countries." If it is merely to transfer resources, as has been the case with Saudi Arabia and Venezuela, where it has not benefited significantly the bottom half, then it is a sheer power play, not an equity play.

It is very interesting to note that the U.S. Congress (both the House and the Senate) has made a significant increase this last year in development assistance. But in doing that, it has made it very clear that it wants to go to the poorest countries, and especially to the poor majority within those countries with specific reference to the rural side. So, in effect, Congress is saying, "If you expect us to play a major role in these new structures, the equity at the other end has to be taken into account." How does that get built into the structure?

Finally, the fourth major factor that needs to be taken into account in these new institution-building structures is that whole concepts of development are changing, both in the developed and developing countries. I do believe that in the developed countries we are changing our concept of what it is that we want from our societies. We have had a cultural revolution of sorts that is still in process. I will not belabor it here, but this will ultimately affect

the structures we build. I make this one footnote on food, concerning meat. My nutritionists, whom I most respect, do make the
point that if the United States wants to add another year to its life
expectancy over the next ten years, a change in its meat consumption
habits (at least the way it produces beef from grain intensive to
nongrain intensive) will have more effect than, as one nutritionist
puts it, an extra $50 billion spent on health. So there are some
mixes coming in here.

With regard to developing countries, very clearly there is a
whole new concept, called self-reliance, which is not autarchy,
but does imply a different approach to both development goals and
to external relationships, that will need to be taken into account.

Against this background it seems that, as we look at the world
food situation, the World Food Conference was probably the most
ambitious approach to solve a global problem that has ever yet been
undertaken. What we saw first was a broad consensus on what the
world food goals ought to be over the next ten or fifteen years,
unprecedented as we compared it with the other conferences that
have been held. Second, there was agreement that by 1985 there
should be a massive increase in food production in the developing
countries, a significant shift in existing patterns. In order to do
this, a new set of institutional structures and an increase in resource
flows would have to be agreed upon. Third, a world food reserve
system was needed to somehow avoid the circumstance of violent
price fluctuations in a new interdependent world food system, and
fourth, there was the need for food aid to address the most urgent
human needs.

This unprecedented agreement on goals has not occurred in
other fields. There was, as Martin put it, this whole galaxy of
structures, which, when I first looked at it, I thought was a Rube
Goldberg setup. But as you dissect it, you find that each one of
these structures serves a purpose and that, as Martin has described
in his paper, the World Food Council did meet a set of needs that
FAO did not meet, and probably could not meet, even with significant
reform.

Each one of the structures had some purpose. The International
Fund for Agricultural Development recognized the need for a new
power to get OPEC in, a new way of allowing them to affect the way
funds are used that could not take place if their money went into the
World Bank at this stage or through other existing organizations.
So that fund was created. OPEC gained much greater say in the
voting power.

Each one of the structures served a purpose when one looked
at it, and one can only underline the progress in the food field when
comparing it with what has happened in the energy field. In the long

run, the energy problem and the food problem are parallel. We faced the prospect of a long-range problem in the energy and food fields by the mid- and late 1980s that had to be addressed. Short-term circumstances brought the problem to a crisis stage in the mid-1970s.

In the food field, we have had this feeling of everybody getting together. You pulled in the Russians, you pulled in the Chinese, you pulled in OPEC. The question remains: How do we go ahead? It has to be a global approach.

In the energy field what we really had was, first, an OPEC opening move of confrontation. The Organization for Economic Cooperation and Development (OECD) responded to this, so that when the consumers got together, Luxembourg came to the Washington conference and Brazil was not invited. Since then I have been struck by the fact that there has yet to be a single global assessment of energy that remotely approaches the kind of assessment that was made at the World Food Conference, either by FAO or by the U.S. Department of Agriculture, or by somebody like Les Brown of the World Watch Institute. So far, the energy assessments have all been from the point of view of either project independence type in the United States or OECD project independence type. There has not been a real global assessment of this scene, and very little account taken of meeting the energy needs of the two thirds of the world that is poor.

Therefore, I argue that we have a very major stake in the success of the World Food Conference proposal. It is the most ambitious attempt at global problem solving yet, and if it succeeds it will stand as an example for others. Edwin Martin has properly underlined how do we pull in the USSR and the People's Republic of China to active participation? They both voted for the resolution; they support it in principle. One of the major topics I took up in China was Chinese participation in this apparatus and why they haven't followed through with it. I can come back to that later, because I did this at the same time I was talking to them about their view toward the Seventh Special Session, and how they proposed to follow up in that mix of institution building that would follow.

The final point I shall make is one I have made earlier; what we have seen in the past 24 months is that our administration, sufficiently preoccupied with other problems, has tended to respond to these global issues of institution building only at the very last moment, and the decisions have been made without the kind of staff work for follow-up implementation that is essential if they are to succeed. To the extent that there has been success in the last 24 months in addressing global issues, it has been due in considerable part to the fact that we have had an active private sector working

with Congress. On the whole I would say there has been considerable success, but the real challenge, to me, is how do we,
in the private sector, organize ourselves to address this galaxy of
problems of the next 18 to 24 months, and make the same kind of
contribution? I am quite skeptical of what, in an election period,
an administration would do without pressure from the outside.

DISCUSSION

Luis Escobar

Edwin Martin mentioned that almost no government has nutrition
policies, which is a dramatic fact in the face of the world situation
today where there are so many people living below levels of absolute
poverty. A pertinent question, in this colloquium on the future of
international economic organizations, is what some of the institutions
that do have some leverage on the formulation of their member
countries' economic policies can do to improve this situation. I am
thinking primarily of the World Bank and the regional development
banks. They make loans for projects; they usually attach some
conditions of an economic nature to be complied with by the borrowing
countries before loan approval or before disbursements start or at
different stages of the project.

One could, however, think that a different approach might be
adopted under which these development banks would make an evalua-
tion of the overall development program of a country and would give
assistance toward the financing of such a program rather than for a
particular project, or they could finance a particular project only
when they are satisfied that it is a part of a well-balanced development program. I realize that such an approach would imply that
the international community would pass a value judgment on the
policies of borrowing countries and would decide whether or not
these countries are eligible for international support.

I am fully aware that objections would be raised to such a
suggestion (which is not new and for which I do not claim authorship
rights) on the basis that it would interfere with sovereign rights;
however, let me just say that one could give the same argument
whenever the international organizations are imposing conditions
for project financing under the present techniques. I think it will
be of interest to the colloquium to have your reaction to this topic.

Edwin M. Martin

I don't know. I'm a skeptic by nature, and I must say I'm
pretty skeptical of moving beyond where we are now in this field

for several reasons. In the first place, I think we are still seeing an increase in nationalism and defense of sovereign rights. In the face of that, the international institutions, about which Luis Escobar was talking, are dominated—not only by votes but by personnel, as well as intellectually—by Western interests, or what is seen as Western control or industrialized country control. I think these two factors, taken together, put a very sharp limit on the ability to exercise more economic influence on domestic policies than is being exercised at the moment.

Those political forces, it seems to me, are somewhat buttressed at the present time by their ability to suggest that we do not know what we are doing. What would you recommend as the policy that IMF should demand the United States to follow or the United Kingdom to follow in order to eliminate stag-inflation? My impression is that one of the important characteristics of the present period, as distinct from the 1950s and the early 1960s, is that then we thought we knew what was good economic policy in terms of a domestic program to meet the needs of our peoples, whereas now nobody really is sure what is the right thing to do.

I would call attention to the fact that some of the most sophisticated brains around, operating as members of the staff and as government representatives in OECD, have been struggling for about five years to find out how to control inflation, not just because of high oil prices. And they still have not figured out what the answer is. They haven't achieved any results in that respect, and had not when the oil price increase came. Therefore, I think our credibility in being able to dictate to others what their policies should be, apart from the political problem, is not very good at the moment.

I would like to add with respect to the food question that it is even more difficult in this area to try to dictate policy, politically difficult, than it is overall. You can talk in a real macrosense about the wisdom of controlling inflation and having exchange rates that represent the real value of money, and about the importance of public savings and reducing budget deficits. However, when you start talking about what should be the priority of food production, then you are getting into internal political relationships between sectors of the economy and groups of people, which are much more political and less subject to general economic decision making than are general economic policies. I think it is, therefore, more difficult to intervene on food policy. I would point out that in the United States we have been wrestling with the question of what is the right policy to provide satisfaction both to farmers and to consumers for at least 40 years now, without conspicuous success, except occasionally by accident. Again, our knowledge is somewhat limited.

On the other hand, it is true that, whether right or not, the financial institutions, bilateral and multilateral, do demand as a condition of their lending various changes in domestic policies, for example, in the food field. I have been reading 25 or 30 agriculture investment project papers, long, difficult, cumbersome documents, over the last few weeks. There are a considerable number of requirements laid down that have been accepted for such things as institutional reforms, policy changes with respect to price and subsidies, and so forth. Whether or not they will be complied with, it is too early to say, but there is an attempt around the edges, at least, to improve policy through this mechanism.

If you tried to formalize it on any generalized basis I am sure that in the present political climate the developing countries would insist on an equal right to influence most of the developed countries. They would argue that, although the developed countries have the money and control the money, this shouldn't give them an unbalanced privilege in this respect. I don't think it's going to be an early date when the United States is prepared to let an outside international authority set its minimum price level for wheat, or dictate when U.S. wheatlands should be taken out of production.

At the food conference, there were a few countries bold enough to say that the food crisis was the responsibility of the United States because it tried to enrich its farmers at the expense of the developing-country importers by restricting production—a cartel operation in which the United States, I may say, was not alone. Australia and Canada also joined in this operation, and there were some informal consultation about it. It was as public as OPEC, but privately there was a considerable coordination. The suggested kind of pressure is just not in the cards in my judgment. Subtly, one can persuade and influence, but public mechanisms of control, it seems to me, are unlikely to be accepted at any time in the near future.

Sidney Weintraub

Let me get back to institutions, because what we have heard from the various panelists are some pretty sharp disagreements on the value of some of the new institutions that have grown up in the agricultural field. I am going to ask some pointed questions, but let me give a little background first.

When I first got into some of this business in Latin America I remember reading a study that described where every time anybody perceived a new problem in the agricultural field, whether a farm or pricing or credit or irrigation or fertilizer, they just decided that the old institution was not really very effective, and the solution was to create a new institution. Some years later, as one began to look at the number of new institutions that were created, the conclu-

sion generally was they were not very effective—and it would be best
to get rid of them all and create another new institution.

We went through something of that nature a few years ago in the
war on poverty in the United States. There was some success, but a
lot of experimentation took place, costing a lot of money, with some
success and a good many failures. The point I am making is that
each new institution created, to use a phrase that James Grant used,
did have a purpose. It was designed to meet a specific problem
and its goal was very worthy, and the result, in a good many cases,
was really chaos rather than progress.

On the other hand, the other part of the argument is that people
turn to a new institution because they are certain that the old institution is not going to reform unless it is shaken up completely or a
new institution is formed. I guess, in a way, what I am asking of
James Grant is, why do you think that if you create a new institution
to meet a specific problem there is going to be any more success
than there generally has been in the past? In looking at it the other
way, you said creating new institutions is one of the fundamental
challenges. Does it really make very much difference in meeting
some of these problems whether we have these institutions? Putting
the question of John Schnittker, if you don't want to create new
institutions because they may not be useful, how do you shake up
the present institutions?

James P. Grant

My answer to Sidney Weintraub would be whether or not the new
structures succeed depends in very large part as to whether or not
society—in this case, international society—wants them to succeed.
If you go by analogy to our domestic institutions, I think you can
compare very appropriately the vast mass of institutional structure
changes that we made in the 1930s with those we sought to do in the
mid-1960s with the war on poverty. In the circumstances of the
1930s we had domestically—this is stretching it a bit—something
like the set of problems we now face internationally. The American
working force, particularly the industrial working force, for 15, 20,
or 30 years had been pressing for a new deal, a difference in the
decision-making process by which our society was run, and particularly the industrial sector in which they were a part. They were
looking for unemployment, Social Security, a whole mix of structures
so that they would not be so sensitive to economic fluctuations.

This finally culminated in the 1930s with a new domestic
economic order, which I think has pretty well stuck. Institutions
like the National Labor Relations Board and the various Social

Security institutions have worked, broadly speaking. We had the Office of Economic Opportunity (OEO) in the mid-1960s, and I think what we really had was a presidentially led program that very soon ran into a lack of will, both because of the Vietnam War and the subsequent boom that made this a problem of a minority.

If we look at new institutions in the food and other areas, we have to decide if we really feel strongly enough that we need a major set of new approaches to make the world society work. If that need is felt and shared widely enough, then I say these new institutions will have a role to perform and they will work. On the other hand, if they are like Atalanta's apples, which you throw behind to the pursuer just to buy yourself time until tomorrow, I will say they will not work.

To be pessimistic, I would say that as I look at the administration, I don't see the U.S. government seized with this set of changes with the same imperative nature that we felt in the mid-1930s. I can see more OEO kind of activity. On the hopeful side, I would just say two things. One is that if one looks at the change in thinking that just occurred in the last 24 months inside the U.S. government, even in the State Department, it's a very significant change, and if you project that change of thinking for another 24 or 36 months, it may well be that we will have the kind of change that would make these institutions meaningful. Second, I have been very encouraged by the way much of the private sector and much of Congress reacted to this set of problems, and they really have been very much in the lead over the last 24 months of the administration. If this can continue, I think it is a very hopeful sign.

John Schnittker

A word in response to Weintraub's question of how do you go about reforming institutions. In the context of the recent World Food Conference, if the group were determined to set up some new functions, believing that they were for real, perhaps it was best that they should establish new groups.

At the same time, it seems to me that to bypass FAO and not to undertake to reform it is not a very defensible kind of action. I don't know how to reform FAO, but I do think it would take a great financial and personnel crisis to do it. It needs to be given a new set of objectives. Whoever controls FAO needs to set a five-year plan to reform the agency, and maybe at the end of that five-year plan appoint new executives, new directors-general, who would themselves undertake to reform it.

Edwin M. Martin

May I just comment on this reforming. Going back to the 1930s
(I came to Washington in 1935), the Civil Service Commission data
on federal employment was in complete chaos with all the new
agencies and programs, and I happened to get involved with this
problem. All the bureau heads had been appointed by Theodore
Roosevelt when he was head of the Civil Service Commission 35 to
40 years before and had difficulty keeping up with these new developments. So they established a planning staff and assigned all the
bureau heads to it, giving them each an in-box, but no out-box.
They forgot them and went ahead and did their work.

I think part of the problem of international agencies is that
there is no heart-lung machine with a switch one can pull.

Lincoln Gordon

A very short question, directly related to Edwin Martin's last
comment and related partly to Henry Costanza's introductory
comments, which, of course, are also directly relevant to this
subject. I find myself troubled. James Grant drew the contrast
between tinkering and sort of structural change on this institutional
front. When we get to my panel, there is at least one idea that
would create one new institution but would also abolish two at the
same time, and that would be something new. That would give a
net of minus one.

But Grant's two analogies—the New Deal domestically and the
Bretton Woods system broadly—were both aftermaths of world-
shattering crises. One was the worst war in human history, and
the second was the most destructive economic condition in human
history. That would seem to suggest that if Grant is really talking
about major restructuring, one has to have that kind of crisis first.
Obviously, one of the major short- and middle-term objectives—what
everybody else is doing—is to avoid precisely either of those two
kinds of crises, and it seems to be highly desirable that they be
avoided. There are some people in the world who believe that the
worse, the better, because they want such revolutionary change.
They believe change can only come from drastic crises, and they
are quite prepared to push things over the brink.

Take, for example, population growth; it has the most drastic
effects on national situations. But it is a very slow rising tide,
and since it is never more than at the most 3.5 percent more
population one year than the year before, it is, unfortunately, in
my view, never regarded as critically as it ought to be, and there-

fore it does not engender the right kind of response. People find it very hard to look forward ten or twenty years.

Grant's concern about the overall overload of institutions, it seems to me, is that kind of a phenomenon rather than either a world depression or obviously a world war phenomenon. I myself was troubled by that aspect of Henry Kissinger's speech of September 1 in the Seventh Special Session. He seemed to have a salt or pepper shaker full of new institutions that he was scattering broadside, most of them rather narrow and functional, but some of them clearly duplicating organizations that already exist. One couldn't help wondering whether he was even aware that some of the competing institutions already exist, at least on paper, with precisely the same responsibilities and functions as were suggested in that speech. I wonder whether the question of reform, of tightening up, of trying to find some ways short of either world-shattering depressions or world wars isn't the realistic task with respect to institutional development?

David Pollock

I did want to talk briefly to the broader issue, because it seems to me that Sidney Weintraub's question was not only very pertinent but was also related to your panel, to our subsequent panel, and in fact to the windup as well. Weintraub's question, in brief, seemed to be this: Why should we believe that new international institutions functioning between 1975 and 2000 will be any more relevant and effective than those functioning from 1950 to 1975? In responding to it, I would just like to leave one thought with you, because as I said it also applies to the next two panels, the luncheon address, and then to the final panel. And that is to remember that, from 1950 to 1975, the international institutions did work well, tremendously well in fact. But primarily for one segment of the world. The Bretton Woods institutions and GATT, for example, contributed very much to a highly expansive global growth performance—of trade, production, and employment—but this phenomenon was much more pronounced for the developed than the developing countries, with a few noticeable exceptions. The institutions I mentioned did their jobs exceptionally well, in terms of stimulating global trade, resource transfers, and balance of payments adjustments. For whatever reason, however, the gains accrued substantially more to the industrialized than to the developing trading nations of the world. OECD Annual Reviews will bear out this last statement, which is factual, not a value judgment.

I think we should recast our minds on the panels dealing with food, with resources, and with trade, and then ask the following

question, which is my rephrasing of Weintraub's question: During
the next 25 years, should there not be a shift in emphasis within
international institutions so that their policies are aimed especially
at the development of developing countries? We have to rethink the
problems that are constantly being posed to Congress, and the
criticisms we so often hear, including in this colloquium, about
malfunctioning institutions. We have to rethink our respective
Washington scenarios, and try to put ourselves into the minds of
those who were at the Seventh Special Session of the UN General
Assembly trying to get agreement on a so-called consensus resolution. They were really thinking about international institutions in
a totally different way. They were thinking about the less-advantaged
3 billion people in this world who are trying to live on incomes of
perhaps 50 cents a day, or much less than that. I would like our
panel to keep those thoughts in mind, because I do think the international institutional system worked incredibly well for one segment
of the world over the past 25 years. But not by the same extent for
the other segment.

Willis Armstrong

The one thing I do not find enough of in the discussions on food
is reference to the problem of sufficient incentives to people to
produce the kinds and amounts of food that obviously a doubling
population is going to require if it is going to stay alive. I realize
that in the World Food Congress and in all the subsequent work that
has been going on, there has been a good deal of emphasis on
switching priorities on the importance of providing the right kind
of stimulation.

Having started in public life as an expert (so to speak) on the
Soviet Union, I have been watching its agricultural performance for
some 35 years. There is a marvelous example of good basic
agronomy, perfectly good soil, somewhat variable weather system,
and a result that is and has been very disappointing in terms of the
utilization of resources or the production of goods. Apparently,
the one way in which this is going to be dealt with is by U.S. agreement with the Soviet Union. But is there any relationship between
international institution building, or international institution fiddling
and the essential problem of the production of food and the application of new technology to productivity in agriculture?

I could take off also on the meat question, and say, "Well, you
know, if you are going to cut down on meat, why don't we cut out
tobacco, which nobody eats, and various other things." But, to go
back to the fundamental question of production and productivity and
institutions, how do you see this?

Edwin M. Martin

I think this goes back to Luis Escobar's point, namely, that the principal negotiating issue between donors and developing countries is the priority given by developing countries to agriculture through their price, tax, investment, personnel assignment, policies, and so on. This is the constant subject of negotiation back and forth. I think that the main problem people face is finding new ways to influence their decisions just on this question of the incentives.

Research is going rather well. The new technologies exist. But farmers are not going to adopt them with the additional risks, the additional cash inputs that are required, unless they have an assurance about the return that they will get. The real revolutions have come about when, for one reason or another, there were very favorable cost-income relationships. This is the central issue that we have to work at.

From the standpoint of the developing country, this is the kind of political issue I had in mind when I talked about the difficulty in changing sectorial priorities from the outside. The urban population, for example, has two great importances to the developing countries. One, it is the urban people who can upset a government who are a social threat, not the countryside. This is why Che Gueverra failed; he misread the whole Cuban situation in this respect. The urban population is the threat.

Second, it is the urban population that produces industrial goods on which they have set their heart as a way of becoming a modern power. They want most to export industrial goods and increase import substitution. Cheap food for the urban workers is essential to be competitive. For both these reasons, the political pressure on the governments is in favor of the urban consumer against the farm producer. So a major role of the international institutions begins to outweigh that pressure. We are constantly seeking means of doing it. It is a subject that will be very important in CGFPI. There is no point in investing in irrigation if the farmer cannot afford the inputs to go with the water, to use it efficiently. So this is a central issue. You have put your finger on it.

I want to give James Grant time to say a little more about China.

James P. Grant

I was in China most of the past three weeks with a group of ostensible leaders from world affairs organizations. Cy Vance*

---

*Cyrus Vance, presently partner with Simpson and Thatcher, formerly World Affairs Leaders of U.S.-China Relations.

was our chairman, which gave us entree with Chinese leaders to discuss their international approach to international issues. The area that I took on for myself was their relationship to these global issues in the economic field.

As you look at the Chinese position, it becomes very clear that two years ago there were two simple postures they threw out. One was self-reliance; countries ought to be self-reliant because China had been. The second was that interdependence was a new word for economic imperialism by the developed countries. This was the way they were going to maintain control of the developing countries and that was the word being used by the United States.

They claimed the Russians were talking about specialization of production and the law of comparative advantage. This was the new Russian way of trying to maintain dominance over the world.

Well, in the past two years there has been a shift in their posture on both of these positions. On self-reliance, they have begun to admit that other countries that are smaller than they have to be much more dependent on the international system; this is a relative sort of question. They held that foreign aid is acceptable as long as it is taken under the eight principles Chou En Lai set forth in the mid-1960s, bringing their term of self-reliance much closer to its use by some of the third-world leaders generally in different parts of the world.

Second, on interdependence, they have agreed that the market economy countries are interdependent, but they feel it is an interdependence of the horse and rider, and that everybody knows who the horse works for, and the first- and second-world countries (their definition of the first world is the USSR and the United States and the second world is all the other industrialized countries: Japan and Western Europe) are the rider in this case.

In this context, initially, they implied that interdependence was always bad, but then, as the New International Economic Order (NIEO) demands came forth, they began to support those demands very vigorously, and the implication was that there can be a good form of interdependence. Then they went on to say that the first and second worlds had to move from confrontation with the developing countries to dialogue. These were the key words: confrontation to dialogue.

Beginning late last spring, after the Lome convention, they began to put out nice sounding words that parts of the second world were beginning to dialogue and that the United States ought to emulate the model of the second world in beginning this dialogue. And so the speech that the minister of foreign trade gave at the Seventh Special Session followed the traditional line: interdependence is bad—horse and rider; but the second world is beginning to dialogue—we should emulate.

Interestingly enough, after the Moynihan-Kissinger speech of September 1, which represented about a 140-degree shift in the U.S. position and was in some ways ahead of the Europeans in approaching the north-south issues, the minister of foreign affairs gave his speech to the General Assembly (a week after the special session) and his speech was identical to the speech that had been given two weeks earlier. They were not able to respond to the concluding findings of the special session.

So my question to them, on a variety of different levels, was now that, according to the resolution of the United Nations, we are all beginning to dialogue, how does the People's Republic of China react to this, and how does it plan to participate in the next round of discussions that the Seventh Special Session had come up with, a series of inner circle forums of which it was not a part. The World Bank, IMF, Development Assistance Committee, the Paris producer-consumer forum—the Chinese, except for the UNCTAD forum, were not a part of any of these.

Their response indicated very clearly that they really had not thought it out. At each echelon, they passed on this question. They did not know how to answer it. The foreign minister replied that in each case they would look at circumstances and then act. When we discussed this with the acting prime minister, Teng Hsiao-P'ing, he gave the same answer.

This then led to a discussion back to the World Food Conference. We said: "You voted for the final resolution of the World Food Conference, just as you voted for the final resolution of the Seventh Special Session, but when the issue came up of your participating in the implementation of the World Food Conference resolutions, and you were offered a seat on the World Food Council by the Group of 77, you bowed out. And you bowed out despite the fact that you are the world's largest importer of fertilizer, the world's largest buyer of fertilizer technology, one of the world's larger importers of food, as well as a major food exporter of rice."

Their response was slightly disorganized. The vice-premier indicated, in effect, that they probably should have been in on this. This ties in with what actually happened: When the Group of 77 asked them if they wanted their seat, the initial response was no. A day or two before the actual conference, their reply was yes, they wanted to sit on the World Food Council. But it was too late to include them at that stage because the Group of 77 had already made the allotments.

It turned out that, on the Chinese side, the Ministry of Agriculture has been given the job of following up on the World Food Conference resolutions; very much as our own USDA, they really do not have a very great interest in the global approach to this set of problems. The Ministry of Agriculture, as it turned out subsequently, was not interested in sticking with this set of issues, and by the time the Ministry of Foreign Affairs had had a chance to look into this, it was too late to get aboard.

And the response of the premier and acting prime minister to this whole set of things was to say, "We obviously need to think more about this." He was going to have some studies made in this field. This is a long way of saying that the Chinese have taken the posture that dialogue is a good thing, it is what we ought to do, and commending what the second world has been doing. If there is an aggressive pursuit of the resolutions of the Seventh Special Session, I think the chances of pulling the Chinese into at least a benign role in this process are somewhere in the ballpark, if it is followed intelligently by the United States and other industrial powers.

It does also mean, however, that the Chinese themselves are institutionally inside their government much less well organized to approach this set of issues than even we are in our own government. And, clearly, one of the things that they need to do—and this could be the purpose of certain dialogues over the next year with them— is to learn how to organize to participate more effectively in this set of processes.

All the issues we have raised with the Chinese have been, if you want to call it, bilateral issues, with the exception of some of the nuclear issues that have been global in scope. The questions concerning the future situation, and food reserves, were a very new set of questions as far as they were concerned, and one in which they have been, as I indicated, responding very, very slowly. One of the interesting facets of this was that the day after Teng Hsiao-P'ing said that they would have to think about it, I had a series of people riding in my cars for the next 48 hours, going to and from different ministries, trying to find out what all this meant. Clearly, somebody was preparing a paper to go back to the acting prime minister on this set of issues.

Edwin M. Martin

On that question, I would just add that during the preparation for the World Food Conference we did try, as did the United States, to get into a dialogue concerning questions about things like food reserves and the future situation, and the Chinese took the documents, were very friendly, and said they had sent them to Peking. No response ever came. It went the same way on our consultative group. We invited them to participate. The U.N. delegation agreed to convey the documents to Peking, but said we should not expect a reply.

III

PROSPECTS FOR INTERNATIONAL ORGANIZATIONS IN THE AREA OF NATURAL RESOURCES

5

NATURAL RESOURCES
AND THE INTERNATIONAL
ECONOMIC ORDER
Lincoln Gordon

This paper is concerned with international institutions involved in the discovery, production, and trade in natural resources, other than food and fuels. Its scope, therefore, includes mineral raw materials and nonfood agricultural and forest products.

BACKGROUND AND UNDERLYING ISSUES

Before exploring the role of international organizations in the natural resource area, it is necessary to survey briefly the factual background and to define the range of problems requiring organized international attention. The widespread current belief that international resource matters have recently entered an entirely new kind of era makes it especially important to identify elements of continuity and of change.

Physical Availability and Resource Depletion

The enormous publicity given in 1972 to the Meadows (or MIT) "First Report" to the Club of Rome,[1] reinforced by such widely read essays as Robert Heilbroner's The Human Prospect,[2] have left a large residue of belief—even in normally well-informed circles—that worldwide economic growth must be limited in the fairly near future because of the exhaustion of a number of essential depletable materials.

In its computerized image of "overshoot and collapse" within the next century, the Meadows report found resource exhaustion

to be the tightest constraint on continued economic growth, followed
shortly by pollution. A logical inference from that prospect would
be increasing international tension and conflict over natural resource
supplies, perhaps leading to the creation of new international institutions for their equitable allocation, for suppressing wasteful uses,
and for ensuring that their scarcity would not cripple the further
development of the poorer countries. Although it had absolutely
nothing to do with short-term physical supply limitations, the success
of the Organization of Petroleum Exporting Countries (OPEC) in
imposing political embargoes in late 1973 and in quadrupling the
level of oil prices had the psychological effect, however illogical,
of strengthening concern about resource exhaustion in general.

   This set of beliefs and concerns is factually unfounded. Except
for oil and gas, where physical exhaustion of recoverable supplies
is a real prospect within the coming 30 to 50 years, physical availability is simply not a problem, provided that substitute forms of
energy can be secured. If necessary, coal alone could meet world
energy needs for well over a century, which seems more than
sufficient time for the development of solar energy, controlled
nuclear fusion, or adequately safe and secure nuclear fission as
almost permanent energy sources within tolerable cost dimensions.
Other minerals are either available in fairly concentrated form for
many thousands or millions of years or can be replaced by substitutes
in ample supply at only slightly higher costs.[3] Moreover, most
minerals, unlike fuels, are not destroyed by use and can be recycled.
(A few uses, such as lead in high octane gasoline, disperse the
mineral beyond recall. Recycling can never be total, but for the
scarcer nonferrous metals and ferroalloys, recycling could be
carried much farther than present practice if increasing costs of
virgin minerals made such a shift economically advantageous.)

   Contrary to the popular current mythology, there is better
reason to be concerned about the adequacy of physical supplies of
certain renewable resources than about so-called "depletables."
Fresh water in many areas, some kinds of timber, and food in
South Asia and tropical Africa (although not worldwide) are the
most obvious cases in point.

   The errors of fact, interpretation, and methodology on the
subject of resource exhaustion in the Meadows report have been
repeatedly documented,[4] and recognition of those errors is gradually
seeping into general public consciousness. Heilbroner publicly has
acknowledged his error on this front,[5] although, somewhat oddly,
he remains unshaken in the conclusions he drew from partly
erroneous premises.

Actual Availability

Physical availability in the earth's crust does not automatically signify availability for use. Actual availability depends on functioning arrangements for exploration, production, and trade. In all these respects, there are significant discontinuities from the practices gradually built up since the industrial revolution and prevailing until the Second World War.

Increasing Internationalization

Even though outpaced by the growth in manufactured goods, international trade in natural resources has shown a prodigious increase in the postwar period (see Table 5.1). Since 1973, there has been a large increase in the nominal values of foreign trade, owing to general inflation and the large increases in food and oil prices, but the volume of trade has fallen off because of the economic recession in the industrial countries.

Two factors combined to produce this result. The industrialized regions of the world enjoyed sustained economic growth more rapid than any in their previous history. The highest growth rates were in Japan and Western Europe, precisely the areas most dependent on natural resource imports. At the same time, for most materials, the United States continued the trend, noted 24 years ago by the Paley Commission,[6] toward increasing import dependence (see Table 5.2). In addition, although still small in absolute volume, a number of the "middle class" developing countries, such as Mexico, Brazil, Venezuela, Korea, and Taiwan, are also entering world markets as significant raw material importers.

Sources of Supply

Contrary to another widely held belief, the source of most international trade in natural resources, other than oil and tropical foods and forest products, is not the developing countries, but rather the resource-rich industrialized countries, such as Canada, Australia, South Africa, and the United States, with the USSR growing in importance. Excluding food and fuel, members of OECD (Organization for Economic Cooperation and Development) accounted in 1973 for about 58 percent of natural resource exports and the Communist countries (mainly the USSR) for about 1 percent, leaving the develop-

TABLE 5.1

The Growth of World Trade
(billions of U.S. dollars at 1972 prices[a])

	Total Exports	Primary Commodities[b]	Primary Commodities, Excluding Food and Fuel[c]
1955	122.9	66.9	25.7
1960	163.7	79.1	30.3
1965	235.3	101.3	35.5
1971	367.6	130.9	40.4
1972	414.7	146.0	45.1
1973	486.2	179.2	56.2
Volume growth 1955-73			
Ratio	×4.0	×2.7	×2.2
Annual rate (percent)	7.9	5.6	4.4

[a]Current values converted to 1972 dollar prices by applying average of U.S. gross national product implicit price deflators for exports and imports.

[b]Includes the following commodity codes in the UN Standard International Trade Classification (SITC):

SITC 0 — Food and live animals
SITC 1 — Beverages and tobacco
SITC 2 — Crude inedible materials, but including SITC 22 (oil seeds, nuts, and kernels)
SITC 3 — Mineral fuels
SITC 4 — Fats and oils (animal and vegetable)
SITC 68 — Nonferrous metals

[c]SITC 2, excluding SITC 22; and SITC 68.

Sources: Calculated from data in GATT, International Trade, 1962, 1972, 1973-74; UNCTAD, Handbook of International Trade and Development Statistics, 1969.

TABLE 5.2

Changing Import Requirements
of the United States
(net imports[a] as percent of domestic use)

	1950	1960	1970
Ferrous metals			
Iron ore	5	25	30
Chromium	100	94	100
Cobalt	92	75	96
Columbium	100	100	100
Manganese	77	92	94
Nickel	99	88	91
Tungsten	80	40	c
Vanadium	b	41	1
Nonferrous metals			
Aluminum (bauxite)	71	77	86
Beryllium	89	96	b
Copper	35	9	8
Lead	59	59	40
Magnesium	0	1	0
Mercury	92	36	38
Platinum	91	95	98
Tin	100	100	100
Titanium	32	30	47
Zinc	37	54	60
Other basic materials			
Petroleum	8	17	22
Natural gas	0	1	3
Uranium	–	47	0
Timber products[d]	11	11	8
Natural rubber	100	100	100

[a]Net imports include semirefined forms, for example, ferro-manganese.
[b]Withheld for disclosure reasons.
[c]Stockpile transactions distort proportions.
[d]Net imports in 1972 are up 50 percent from 1970.

Source: Final Report of the National Commission on Materials Policy (Washington, D.C., June 1973), pp. 2-23.

TABLE 5.3

Share of Developing Countries in World
Exports of Primary Commodities
(billions of U.S. dollars at current prices)

	1955	1960	1970	1973
All primary commodities[a]	49.7	60.8	114.7	208.8
Developing countries' share (percent)	43	40	39	41
Food[b]	20.4	24.8	45.6	85.5
Developing countries' share (percent)	43	37	32	27
Fuel[c]	10.2	12.7	28.3	63.1
Developing countries' share (percent)	54	56	63	68
Primary commodities[d] excluding food and fuel	19.1	23.3	40.8	60.2
Developing countries' share (percent)	38	34	30	31

[a]SITC 0, 1, 2, 3, 4, 68 (see Table 5.1 for definitions).
[b]SITC 0, 1, 22, and 4.
[c]SITC 3.
[d]SITC 2 (excluding 22) and 68.

Sources: UN, Monthly Bulletin of Statistics (July 1974);
UNCTAD, Handbook of International Trade and Development Statistics,
1969; and Review of the World Commodity Situation and Report on
International Action on Individual Commodities, UNCTAD,
TB/B/C.1/174 (January 1975).

ing countries responsible for only 31 percent.* Their share has
shown a declining trend, falling between 1955 and 1973 from 43 to
41 percent for primary commodities as a whole and from 38 to 31
percent for primary products other than food and fuel (see Table 5.3).

---

*Since 1973, the large increases in oil prices have increased
greatly the weighting of fuels in the value of world trade as a whole,
thereby increasing the apparent share of the developing countries.
The benefits, of course, have accrued to the few oil-exporting nations
within the developing country category. For the purposes of this
paper, the data prior to the oil price increases of 1973-75 present
a more relevant perspective.

The confusion on this point arises from the fact that exports of primary commodities still account for the overwhelming proportion of total developing country exports and are therefore of transcendent importance to their foreign exchange earnings and development prospects. From the viewpoint of industrialized countries, however, developing country supplies are less consequential than is generally supposed. That is even more true in relation to total production, including domestic production in the industrialized countries as well as imports from abroad (see Table 5.4).

Arrangements for Exploration and Production

Until World War II, exploration, production, processing, and trade in natural resources were almost entirely controlled by transnational companies based in Western Europe and North America. Mineral production in developing countries was generally carried on in company enclaves, with payment of modest royalties to the host government but otherwise complete technical and commercial control by the mining companies. Some materials were processed to higher stages by the same companies, while others were traded on markets in London or New York. Except in wartime, the industrial consuming countries had little concern about access to supplies and the host country governments were in no position to affect either quantities or prices significantly. In countries like Canada and Australia, foreign capital (mainly American and British, with Japanese invest- ment growing in importance in Australia) also played a large part in minerals development, along with some domestic participation, but foreign investment was warmly welcomed as a means of accelera- ting economic development and there was little interference with the companies beyond general and nondiscriminatory taxation.

The end of colonialism in the developing world, followed by a surge of nationalism in Asia and Africa that was also paralleled in earlier independent Latin America (and even nowadays in Canada and Australia), has put an end to that set of traditional arrange- ments. That is one of the sharp discontinuities in the international economic order. Thus far, no stable arrangements have been developed to take their place, either through direct negotiation between mining (and rubber, timber, and fiber) companies and the host governments concerned or under the guidance of international organizations. As a result, political uncertainty is at least on a par with economic considerations in determining the amounts and location of natural resource investments. There is good reason to believe that one cause of the declining developing countries' share in natural resource exports has been a company preference for expansion in politically "safer" areas, even when the ore qualities

TABLE 5.4

Developing Country Exports in Relation to World Production and World Exports of Selected Commodities, 1970-73

	Developing Country Exports in Proportion to:	
	World Production (percent)	World Exports (percent)
Petroleum, crude	49	91
Timber	2	25
Copper	31	54
Wheat	1	3
Coffee	69	96
Sugar	19	71
Cotton	18	56
Iron ore	16	37
Beef	1	29
Maize (corn)	3	23
Tobacco	11	26
Wool	11	20
Rice	1	39
Rubber, natural	90	97
Zinc	9	24
Cocoa	78	100
Tin	75	86
Tea	48	83
Bauxite	29	73

Sources: ABMS, Yearbook of the American Bureau of Metal Statistics; FAO, Production Yearbook, 1974, Trade Yearbook, 1974, Commodity Review and Outlook, 1973-74; IBRD, Commodity Trade and Price Trends, 1973, 1974; E. Stern and W. Tims, "The Relative Bargaining Strengths of the Developing Countries," in Changing Resource Problems of the Fourth World, Ronald Ridker, ed., Johns Hopkins University Press for Resources for the Future, Washington, D.C., 1976; Metallgesellschaft, Metal Statistics, 1963-73; OECD, Statistics of Foreign Trade: Trade by Commodities (Series C), 1972, 1973; and the UN Statistical Office, Commodity Imports: Share of the Developing Countries in the Imports of Principal Trading Nations, vol. 3, 1967.

are superior or the basic production costs lower in the developing countries.

Producer Cooperation

The fabulous success of OPEC in raising oil prices and the revenues of the oil exporters has stimulated a tremendous interest (producers' hopes and importers' fears) in the possibility of other producer cartels. Cartels generally had been in low repute since the collapse of the classic prewar efforts in producer stabilization of the natural rubber and coffee markets. New producer organizations have been formed in copper (Inter-Governmental Council of Copper Exporting Countries [CIPEC], 1967), bauxite (International Bauxite Association [IBA], 1974), and iron ore (Association for Iron Ore Exporting Countries [AIOEC], 1975), and there has been tentative discussion of new forms of cooperation among governments of countries exporting natural rubber and tungsten, as well as several food products. Some Western observers two years ago, at the height of the commodity price boom, foresaw substantial success in cartel efforts, characterizing them as part of the "threat from the third world."[7] In this author's view, the possibilities are quite limited. The case of oil is unique for a number of critical reasons.

Without ruling out entirely the possibility of other cases of joint action by producers to raise prices and control the volume of exports, it can be said with confidence that no other commodity is a true analog of oil—in the scale of potential price increases, the impact on consumers, or the effects on the world economy. In the early 1970s, among the nonfood items, only timber, copper, cotton, iron ore, coal, wool, synthetic fibers, and rubber reached an annual international trade volume of over $1 billion per year, and none exceeded $5 billion. Hides and skins, zinc, tin, and bauxite-alumina in combination ran between $500 million and $1 billion. Trade in oil was then running at about $27 billion per year, and since 1973 exceeds $100 billion.

The scope for price increases in the nonfood and fuel commodities is limited by possibilities of substitution, either in source or in use. Aluminum is a potential substitute for copper in most uses and for steel in many, and it can be extracted from kaolin clays, alunite, anorthosite, laterite, or other ores widely present in industrialized countries at costs around 25 percent above bauxite and in far less time than it takes to replace oil. The Korean War experience in saving tungsten through the use of tungsten carbide and other substitutes is a dramatic illustration.[8] Our generation has witnessed a whole family of new synthetic substitutes for natural rubber, cotton, silk, and wool, and for metals generally by concrete and plastics. Fiberglass may soon replace copper in some electrical uses.

Substitution requires time and capital investment, so that temporary opportunities for market manipulation by producers do exist, especially during economic booms in the industrialized countries. Any producer cartel in its right mind, however, must act with caution and realism if it is to avoid the permanent destruction of a large share of its markets. The substantial increases in bauxite prices initiated two years ago by Jamaica, and followed by some other suppliers, are consistent with such caution. They are estimated to translate into only 3 cents per pound of aluminum,[9] scarcely a significant factor in the current worldwide inflation.

Finally, no other commodity presents the unique circumstances of the low population oil producers in the Persian Gulf, whose foreign exchange earnings are far beyond their capacity for current expenditure. In most cases, producing countries cannot afford the unemployment that would result from large curtailments in production or the losses of fiscal revenue that would result from politically motivated embargoes.

Host Government Control of Terms of Production and Sales

The most striking discontinuity since World War II in the field of natural resources is the effective assumption of control over the terms of production, and in many cases of sale, by host country governments. The means employed cover a wide range. At the extreme is outright nationalization, but more common measures include insistence on substantial equity participation, legislative or administrative constraint on profit earnings and remittances, requirements for some degree of upgrading or processing within the country, intervention in the determination of selling prices and destinations, and requirements for the employment of local nationals, the provision of social infrastructure, and shipping on flag vessels of the country concerned.

Nor are such controls limited to developing countries with radical socialist regimes or Communist state-trading countries; they are manifested even in the traditionally "safe" countries, such as Canada and Australia. This true revolution in the locus of effective control is most noticeable in former colonial areas now seeking the affirmative exercise of economic sovereignty, but it also reflects the universal tendencies toward economic nationalism and greater government intervention in a wide range of economic activities.

The Drive for International Management
of Commodities

For a mixture of reasons, commodity policy has become a
major theme of current pressures from the developing countries
for reshaping the international economic order. Their arguments
trace back to the doctrines evolved by Dr. Raul Prebisch at the
Economic Commission for Latin America almost 30 years ago, when
he focused on an alleged long-term deterioration in the terms of
trade of raw material-producing countries as a central feature of
their "peripheral" relationship to the industrialized "center." More
recently, Latin American intellectuals have developed an elaborate
theory of "dependency," in which foreign corporate control of
domestic natural resources plays an important part. Nationalist
fervor is readily focused on the issue of control over natural
resources, exemplified alike in the Brazilian slogan of 1953,
"The Petroleum is Ours," and in the UN General Assembly resolution
on "permanent sovereignty over natural resources" of 1970.[10]

Some form of international organization of commodity markets,
both to reduce fluctuations and to improve remuneration to suppliers,
has been a constant theme of the UN Conference on Trade and Development (UNCTAD) since its formation in 1964, second only to the drive
for tariff preferences on developing country exports. Beyond doubt,
however, it was OPEC's success in quadrupling oil prices in 1973-74,
coming on the heels of the greatest general commodity price boom
since the early 1950s, which gave this drive its current vigor.
While no objective observer could defend the terms of all the traditional minerals concessions as being fair to the host countries, the
rhetoric employed by developing country spokesmen sometimes
reaches farcical lengths in the other direction, attributing the wealth
of the presently industrialized countries and the poverty of developing
countries entirely to raw material exploitation at unfavorable terms
of trade.

More troublesome than rhetorical forays aimed at remaking
economic history is the substantial danger of disappointed expectations. Internationally managed commodity markets do not hold out
a true prospect of huge additional foreign exchange earnings or
resource transfers to the developing countries. They cannot substitute for the internal structural changes that are at the core of real
development. On the other hand, consumers as well as producers
have something significant to gain from the greater price stability
and smoother flows of resources that might result from well-
managed international buffer stock arrangements. In the case of
grains, there is now an official worldwide consensus in support of
international reserve stocks, even though its implementation has
yet to be realized. Whatever the objective merits, however, the

intense current political focus on international commodity market management is an important factor affecting international institutional development in this field.

INTERNATIONAL ORGANIZATIONS CONCERNED WITH NATURAL RESOURCES

The circumstances outlined in the previous section—physical, economic, and political—give rise to four problem areas involving natural resources that are presently the concern of a wide variety of international institutions: the discovery and development of supplies, the conditions of trade, the international organization of markets, and international compensatory financing for shortfalls in commodity export earnings. There is some overlap among all of these categories. For example, the organization of a particular raw material market, with international buffer stocks designed to reduce price fluctuations, would also affect the conditions of trade, might promote or retard the development of supplies, and would dampen fluctuations in earnings and reduce the claims for compensatory financing. Nevertheless, the four categories differ in the kinds of problems and possible actions involved, and therefore in the kinds of international organization best suited to each.

Surveying the array of international institutions involved in these four areas, one finds them ranging from the most general to the highly specific, from global to regional to functional, from high policy to purely technical, and from balanced representation of various interests to advocacy of a particular set of interests.

Resource questions occupy a substantial fraction of the time of the UN General Assembly's Committee II and the Economic and Social Council (ECOSOC), with its Committee on Natural Resources. A modest data-collecting and analytic capacity is provided by the Center for Natural Resources, Energy and Transport in the central Secretariat in New York. Since 1964, functional UN bodies with substantial interest in resource matters have included the UN Conference on Trade and Development (UNCTAD), the UN Development Program (UNDP), the UN Environmental Program (UNEP), the UN Educational, Scientific, and Cultural Organization (UNESCO), the UN Industrial Development Organization (UNIDO), and the Food and Agriculture Organization (FAO). All these bodies possess or are open to substantially universal membership. Resource questions are also within the province of other institutions of more limited membership loosely related to the UN system, including the General Agreement on Tariffs and Trade (GATT), the International Atomic Energy Agency (IAEA), the World Bank Group, including the Inter-

national Finance Corporation (IFC), the International Monetary Fund
(IMF), and the regional development banks for Latin America,
Asia, and Africa. The regional economic commissions of the UN
also deal with resource matters, giving increasing attention in
recent years to the training of resource specialists, resource
exploration, and planning for resource development.

Relevant institutions of still more limited membership include
the Organization for Economic Cooperation and Development (OECD),
the (British) Commonwealth, and the European Community. Then
there are the formally organized producer-consumer commodity
groups, each with its autonomous council, for wheat, tin, cocoa,
coffee, sugar, and so on; a number of specialized commodity groups;
commodity organizations composed only of exporting country members
for oil (OPEC), bauxite (IBA), copper (CIPEC), bananas, and iron
ore (AIOEC); and one organization of resource consumers, the
International Energy Agency (IEA). A new entrant into the field,
with uncertain but potentially great significance, is the Conference on
International Economic Cooperation (IEC), growing out of the international energy discussions in Paris, which took shape late in 1965
as an organization of 27 members. It represents the three major
groups of industrialized countries, oil exporters, and non-oil-
exporting developing countries. The group has set up four commissions of 15 members each, dealing, respectively, with energy, raw
materials, development, and finance.

If anyone still believes that the central purpose of international
organization should be efficient decision making and tidy administration, he will find a tabulation of these institutions and their various
involvements in resource matters deeply dismaying. More realistic
students of institutional behavior, sensitive to the diverse political
interests and bureaucratic pressures at stake, will also recognize
that the pattern contains duplications, overlaps, and gaps that can
only be explained in terms of each agency's particular history. It
is a striking gap that the United Nations system contains no body
with a specialized interest in international energy issues, apart
from the IAEA. Another gap, but one that will presumably be filled
somehow as an outcome of the Conference on the Law of the Seas,
is the lack of an international agency dealing with seabed resources.
For historic reasons, the two most active institutions in the commodity trade field, GATT and UNCTAD, were both somewhat irregular
in their origin: the former a supposedly provisional residue of the
Havana negotiations for an international trade organization and the
latter a permanent secretariat for a periodic intergovernmental
conference that has most of the attributes, but not the formal status,
of a UN specialized agency.

To trace the historic evolution even of these two institutions, to say nothing of the many others already named, would unduly extend the scope of this paper.[11] It may be useful, however, to summarize briefly who does what in relation to the four functions outlined above.

Resource Supply Development

In the field of resource supply development, the United Nations Development Program (UNDP) over the years has given special emphasis to resource surveys—geological, soil, and forest—in continuation of a principal objective of the predecessor UN Special Fund. UNDP has also supported the creation of national geological survey agencies and the training of technical personnel. A new institution in this field, nominally independent but to be administered by UNDP during its first four years, is the UN Revolving Fund for Natural Resource Exploration. Financed by voluntary contributions of a few million dollars, the Fund is to focus on the phase of resource development between broad geological surveys and the costly, detailed feasibility studies that traditionally are the responsibility of mining enterprises.

Other UN agencies support basic and applied scientific research and training related to natural resource discovery and development. They include UNESCO and the five regional economic commissions; UNEP with respect to environmental implications and possible "outer limits"; IAEA for uranium and for application of nuclear science to the discovery and development of other minerals; and FAO for all aspects of agricultural and forest resources. UNIDO has an active interest in mineral supplies for nascent metallurgical industries and in the encouragement of higher processing of raw materials within developing countries. The central UN Secretariat and the International Law Commission also have given some attention to mining legislation.

Although this spate of UN activity is undoubtedly making a significant contribution to the development of technical personnel and sophistication on resource problems, its overall scale is quite modest. Until very recently, international institutions have been little involved in the costly and risky phases of mineral development. These phases have been the traditional province of private mining companies, mainly based in the industrialized world and nowadays supplemented in increasing measure by state-owned or mixed ventures in many of the developing countries. The World Bank Group has deliberately limited its involvement, so that its direct financial contributions to mining investments in developing countries have amounted to less than 2 percent of all foreign financing for this purpose in the past two decades. The Bank has financed related infrastructure investments in transportation and power, but it has eschewed most direct mining investment on the grounds that private capital is available on reasonable terms.

In 1973, the Bank management recommended a greatly enlarged role for the group in mineral exploration and development through loans both to state-owned and mixed ventures and to private projects where international institutional participation might help serve as a buffer between the companies and the host governments. Except for enlarged participation by IFC in joint ventures combining domestic (state, private, or mixed) companies with foreign companies, these proposals were not approved by the executive board.

In his address of September 1, 1975, to the Seventh Special Session of the UN General Assembly, Secretary Henry Kissinger appeared to indicate some modification in the preexisting U.S. hesitancy on this front, proposing "a major new international effort to expand raw material resources in developing countries," in which the World Bank and its affiliates, "in concert with private sources, should play a fundamental role." Recognizing that private foreign investment is no longer as welcomed or as interested as in the past, he specifically endorsed the concept of a buffer role for the World Bank Group.

The sensitivity of this topic, however, is such that the resolution adopted by consensus on September 16 made no explicit reference to natural resource development. It did call for increased financial support for the World Bank Group (especially the International Development Association) and for UNDP and the regional development banks. For IFC, it endorsed only "consideration . . . to the expansion of IFC capital without prejudice to the increase in resources of other . . . institutions." And on the buffer role, it stated, in highly negotiated and quite obscure terms: "to the extent desirable, the World Bank Group is invited to consider new ways of supplementing its financing with private management, skills, technology and capital and also new approaches to increased financing of development in developing countries, in accordance with their national plans and priorities." A later paragraph called on "appropriate United Nations bodies and other related intergovernmental agencies . . . to examine ways and means of increasing the flow of public and private resources to developing countries, including proposals made at this session to provide investment in private and public enterprises in developing countries."

These noncommittal conclusions reflect the failure of the international community to achieve real consensus on the role of private enterprise in resource development. ECOSOC's essay in that direction through the "Group of Eminent Persons on Multinational Corporations" may have set the cause back rather than advancing it. Nor is it aided by the reiterated endorsement in developing country conferences of the one-sided principles of "permanent sovereignty" over natural resources. Secretary Kissinger's September 1 address included a vigorous and lengthy plea for a new step toward an agreed statement of principles on treatment of what are now called "transnational enterprises," but the topic went unmentioned in the final resolution. It does, however, remain on the active agenda of UNCTAD, the UN Commission on Transnational Corporations, OECD, and other public and private international bodies. Actual progress, if any, seems more likely to emerge in the near future from experimentation in new forms of agreement between individual companies and host governments.

The functional organizations for individual commodities are generally more concerned with conditions of trade and potential oversupply than with resource development. Some of them, however, have given attention to technical measures to improve production efficiency and to strengthen the competitive position of their commodities against potential substitutes. Mention should also be made of a prospective new international organization for resource development, the International Sea-bed Authority under discussion at the ongoing Conference on the Law of the Sea.

Conditions of Trade

Two international institutions, GATT and UNCTAD, predominate in the field of conditions of trade in raw materials. By "conditions of trade" is meant the terms and international rules governing access to markets and (potentially if not actually) access to supplies. As the negotiating forum for formal contractual international agreements on tariffs and nontariff barriers, with at least a rudimentary system of sanctions to enforce compliance, GATT is the major actor. The current Multilateral Trade Negotiations (MTN)(Tokyo Round), like their predecessors, will be mainly concerned with trade in manufactured goods and temperate agricultural products, but they will also devote substantial attention to natural resources, including the critical issue of tariff escalation, which discourages the higher processing of raw materials in countries of origin. There is also a fair prospect that the Tokyo Round may introduce new rules governing export restrictions in times of scarcity, thus initiating a degree of international law on access to supplies.

Since its creation in 1964, UNCTAD also has constituted a major international forum for discussion of the conditions of trade, in raw materials as well as in manufactured goods. UNCTAD's central concern is the interest of poorer countries in expanded trade as an instrument for economic development. In contrast to GATT, UNCTAD has been a forum more for debate than negotiation, but it has brought about generalized acceptance for the principle of nonreciprocal trade preferences for developing countries and also has become the sponsor of negotiations on a number of specific commodity agreements.

In the analytic work of the two staffs and in broader policy discussions, as distinct from detailed negotiations, there is a large overlap between GATT and UNCTAD. There is a modicum of formal collaboration, facilitated by their proximity in Geneva, but at least until recent years their mutual relations have been suspicious and even hostile.

Other international institutions with a tangential impact on conditions of resource trade include FAO for agricultural materials, the European Community both for internal trade and for its preferential arrangements with associated states, and the various commodity study groups for improving market information. What impact, if any, will be made by the Commission on Raw Materials of the new Paris Conference on International Economic Cooperation cannot be foreseen at this writing.

Resource Market Organization

In the area of actual or possible international action to organize resource markets or to intervene in their functioning, the numbers of institutions involved considerably exceed the numbers of working commodity arrangements. In the system of international institutions worked out at the end of World War II under American and British leadership, responsibility for supervising possible commodity arrangements was assigned to the International Trade Organization (ITO), whose charter (Havana, 1948) included a set of guiding principles that are still worth serious consideration. When the ITO charter failed to be ratified, responsibility for a watching brief was transferred to the secretary general of the UN, aided by an Interim Coordinating Committee on International Commodity Agreements. GATT was represented on that body, but with the constitution of UNCTAD in 1964, its Trade and Development Board and Committee on Commodities took over this nominal responsibility.

In theory, when producers or consumers, exporters or importers, and their respective governments feel that an organized arrangement

should be made for a particular commodity, they apply to the United
Nations through UNCTAD for the convening of a commodity conference.
In practice, the individual commodity groups, such as the International Wheat Council and the International Coffee Council, have
been virtually autonomous. UNCTAD, however, has sponsored a
series of negotiations for the establishment of a Cocoa Agreement;
the recent renegotiation of the Tin Agreement was also conducted
under UNCTAD auspices. More broadly, UNCTAD has taken the
lead in recent years in developing an elaborate proposal for an
"integrated program of commodity arrangements," which figured
as a major item on the agenda of the fourth UNCTAD plenary conference in Nairobi in May 1976. FAO is also active in this field, having
sponsored study groups on hard fibers and jute and some other
nonfood products.

With the enhanced interest in commodity arrangements during
the past few years, other international agencies also have entered
the field. The International Monetary Fund (IMF) established a lending facility for buffer stocks in 1969, which has been used on a
modest scale to finance some producing country contributions (mainly
Bolivia's) to the tin buffer stock, and which might be applied to the
new Cocoa Agreement. Since the borrowing country must be in
balance-of-payment difficulties to be eligible and since the loans
are of only three- to five-year duration, this role of IMF is marginal.
In May 1975, the World Bank management recommended a new
policy of 15-year loans to assist member countries in financing
contributions to the tin buffer stock, but formal approval has not
yet been forthcoming.

Proposals for a major shift in the attitude of industrialized
countries toward commodity arrangements figured in the British
Commonwealth conference in Jamaica in early 1975. Commodity
arrangements are also one of the items for consideration in an
OECD high-level committee on commodities, established in May
of that year. They are bound to be at the center of discussions of
the newly created Commission on Raw Materials of the Paris
Conference on International Economic Cooperation.

At the operating level, specialized commodity councils, representing the interests directly concerned and staffed by experts
familiar with the intricacies of production and marketing, are the
locus of specific negotiations and functional decisions. They typically
represent both producers and consumers, with votes weighted by
importance in production or trade. Whether and to what extent
they should work under the supervision of some more general
commodity agency, and if so where that agency should be placed,
are among the questions for international discussion in the period
ahead. The major working commodity arrangement composed

exclusively of producers is OPEC, which is outside the scope of this paper, but the more recently established producer associations in bauxite, copper, and iron ore are also interested in influencing market organization to improve their earnings and perhaps to bring about more stable market conditions. The sole counterpart organization on the consumer side is the International Energy Agency, formed at U.S. initiative in 1974, but the original intention to make it a collective bargaining agency on prices and supplies has not materialized.

Compensatory Financing

Apart from efforts to improve conditions of trade and to organize resource markets through commodity arrangements, the developing countries for two decades have pressed for some form of automatic international financing, supplementary to regular bilateral and multilateral aid transfers, to compensate for cyclical shortfalls in earnings from exports of primary products. The interest in compensatory financing developed in part because of the reluctance of the industrialized countries to interfere with market operations through commodity agreements, but also from the growing recognition that price stability would not be matched by stability of earnings. Business cycles in consuming countries or weather-induced fluctuations in agricultural supplies can bring about large variations in the volume of resource exports. In the case of agricultural products, assuming demand to be fairly constant and not highly price elastic, earnings might be more stable without price stabilization, since in periods of short supply unit prices are likely to be high.

Insofar as the objective of commodity arrangements is to avoid interference in developmental efforts from fluctuations in foreign exchange earnings, compensatory financing is a better suited instrument than market organization. It can be applied to export earnings from specific individual commodities, a defined group of commodities, or export earnings as a whole. It also avoids windfall gains to rich country exporters. On the other hand, it does nothing to further the interest of consuming or importing countries in limiting price increases in times of shortage and it makes no direct contribution to security of access to supplies, two objectives that could in principle be served by a properly functioning buffer stock arrangement. Strictly speaking, therefore, compensatory financing may be complementary to market organization, with overlapping but different purposes. It falls more in the field of aid resource transfer or developmental policy than resource policy as such.

At the level of debate and discussion, the regional economic commissions of the UN in Latin America, Asia, and Africa, together with UNCTAD since 1964, have been strong proponents of compensatory financing arrangements. Since those agencies have no significant financial resources, the possibilities of action have rested with the two principal financial institutions, IMF and the World Bank. IMF entered this field in 1963 through the creation of a compensatory financing facility for export fluctuations, permitting additional borrowings (since 1966 up to 50 percent of a country's quota) when export earnings fall below a trend line for reasons "largely beyond the control" of the country concerned. About $1.4 billion were borrowed under this arrangement up to the end of 1975. Following several months of discussion in the international financial community, the U.S. government announced in September 1975 its support for a major enlargement and liberalization of this approach. In December, the IMF executive board took action to increase the ceilings on drawings for compensatory financing from 50 to 75 percent of a country's quota (from 25 to 50 percent within any one year), raising the potential total by about $2 billion. It also eased the rules for calculating shortfalls. The prospective increase in IMF quotas by almost one third will further enlarge the scale of potential drawings. The new IMF Trust Fund, financed by profits on the sale of a portion of IMF's gold holdings, will be used to soften repayment terms for the poorest developing countries, including their borrowings for compensatory financing.

Proposals have also been advanced from time to time for supplementary financing by the World Bank on concessionary terms related to export earning fluctuations. The subject was studied jointly with the IMF staff in a 1968-69 review of primary product price stabilization, but the Bank has preferred to focus on more specific activities, such as assistance to primary product diversification and higher processing, consistent with its general resistance to program lending. The increasing participation of IMF in what amounts to developmental lending, in contrast to short-term balance-of-payment problems, entails an increasing overlap between its interests and those of the World Bank. That fact has been recognized through the establishment of a joint Bank-Fund Development Committee.

Finally, mention should be made of the European Community's adoption early in 1975 of a compensatory financing arrangement, known as STABEX, for the 46 associated states from Africa, the Caribbean, and the Pacific (ACP states), a major innovation incorporated in the Lome Convention. STABEX deals mainly with agricultural products (the only mineral included being iron ore), and provides for compensatory loans on a case-by-case basis for short-

falls in export earnings from levels of recent years. For the poorest
ACP countries, the loans need not be repaid; for the others, repayment takes place only when earnings substantially exceed the trend
line. Some observers have seen in the Lome arrangement a possible
precedent for compensatory arrangements on a wider scale.

PROSPECTS AND PROBLEMS FOR
INTERNATIONAL INSTITUTIONS

Against this background of shifting issues of policy and present
institutional arrangements, what are the principal institutional
questions lying ahead? To identify them requires some assumptions
concerning the broader international framework: the likely pattern
of relationships among the Western nations (including Japan,
Australia, and New Zealand as a kind of "Far West"), between
West and South, between West and East, and possibly between East
and South.

For purposes of this discussion, it is assumed that national
governments will continue to be the major actors on the international
stage, with varying degrees of regional and global cooperation but
no significant approach to formal confederation, even within the
European Community. From that assumption, it follows that international institutions will continue to draw their authority from
national governments and be subject to the limitations of each nation's
sovereignty. That does not exclude a role for international management of common enterprises, such as a Sea-bed Authority, a
strengthened International Atomic Energy Agency, or a series of
international commodity buffer stocks. Like the World Bank and
IMF, however, such institutions will be international rather than
supranational in character.

It is also assumed that cooperation among the Western nations
will intensify the interdependence achieved among them since World
War II and will require policy harmonization in an increasing range
of functional areas. Although East-West and East-South economic
relations will grow in importance, it is assumed that the West and
South together will be the major policy makers and negotiators on
international resource matters. Finally, relations between West
and South are expected to continue as an uneasy mixture of confrontation and somewhat suspicious collaboration, but with the
confrontational element diminishing in relation to practical efforts
to find meeting grounds of mutual interest. One common objective
will be the accelerated development of the South, but without a
major transfer of basic wealth or income (as distinct from incremental income) from the West.

It is easy to imagine other plausible scenarios, such as aggressive rivalry for scarce resources among the Western nations,
outright economic warfare between North and South or portions of
both, or Western abandonment of interest in Southern development.
Any of these alternatives would lead to quite different institutional
conclusions from those presented here. They would constitute
unnecessary and costly setbacks to the achievement of widely shared
aspirations, setbacks that are the task of enlightened leadership to
prevent. On the other end of the spectrum, some observers believe
in a much more rapid development of global supranational institutions,
but their scenario seems implausible except as the ultimate product
of a major catastrophe, either natural or man-made.

Within that general framework, each of the functional fields
outlined above raises questions of institutional gaps or indicated
reforms.

Development of Supplies

Here the essential gap lies in the absence of stable and generally
acceptable arrangements for the costly and risky phases of mineral
resource discovery and development, beyond the prefeasibility stage
contemplated by the new UN Revolving Fund. It is simply unclear
today what share of those functions will continue to be performed by
private mining enterprises, on what kind of terms, and with what
arrangements for resolving disputes between them and host country
governments—or what alternative institutions might replace the
mining companies. Since they have unique skills and often special
access to markets, many developing countries would like their
participation, permitting them a fair return on investment but
appropriating any income beyond such a return, project by project.
The mining enterprise tradition, on the other hand, looks to an
occasional bonanza to cover the costs of unsuccessful explorations
and marginal mining. If the companies cannot secure exceptional
returns from the more profitable mines, who will finance the dry
holes? Those developing country governments suspicious of private
enterprise in general would like to see this done by an expanded UN
Revolving Fund or possibly by the World Bank and regional banks.
The needed sums, however, greatly exceed the prospective scale
of UN operations. As to the banks, the industrialized countries are
loath to see public resources devoted to minerals exploration when
private resources could be made available.

What seems required is a framework for sophisticated negotiation between governments and mining companies in which all cards

are laid on the table and a wide spectrum of unforeseeable contingencies is allowed for in advance in the terms of the contracts. Some observers believe that a general code of conduct for transnational enterprises in the extractive industries, with arrangements for third-party arbitration of disputes, would meet this need. It surely does no harm for this possibility to be explored, and the UN Commission on Transnational Corporations provides a forum for doing so. But it is hard to see any reason to alter a skeptical judgment on the prospect for meaningful progress set forth in a paper three years ago: "that the only kinds of international code that could be agreed to formally by LDC governments would by their very nature be unacceptable to the investors."[13] Case-by-case experimentation is a more promising road at this stage. As suggested in the same paper, however, there is a major potential role for the World Bank, IFC, and the regional banks in facilitating such open bilateral negotiations, providing a kind of certificate of mutual benefit in the contractual terms and informally assisting in the resolution of investment disputes. Out of this process there might gradually develop a kind of case law that could be codified when circumstances are more propitious.

The international financial institutions and various UN agencies also have a useful role in improving the sophistication of governments in the least developed mineral-producing countries. At one time, the World and regional banks were reluctant to recognize the legitimacy of state-owned mining enterprises, but that point is scarcely a serious continuing issue.

There is an interrelationship between the issues of supply development and the international organization of markets. Large fluctuations in prices and volume of sales contribute to tension between mining companies and host governments, feeding suspicions of undue profits or of company failure to maintain a host country's market share. If such fluctuations could be limited through effective buffer stock arrangements, one important source of investment disputes would also be reduced.

In the development of some kind of international seabed authority, one may anticipate continuing jockeying among industrialized countries seeking to maximize the opportunities for transnational corporations, developing countries seeking potential income from seabed exploitation, and existing minerals producers fearful of a new source of competition. It now seems probable that coastal states will exercise effective economic sovereignty over 200-mile zones, but beyond that large limit, some kind of new international licensing or managerial agency is evidently required.

Conditions of Trade and Market Structures

These are the areas where the present institutional situation is most confusing. For more than a decade, an uneasy coexistence has prevailed in Geneva between GATT and UNCTAD. The UN General Assembly, ECOSOC, UNIDO, and other agencies make frequent forays into these domains. Now a new entrant is on the horizon in the form of the Paris Conference on International Economic Cooperation, with its commissions on energy, raw materials, development, and financial matters. OECD, the Group of 77, the regional economic commissions, and other international bodies all contribute to the flood of mimeographed paper.

The scene is somewhat reminiscent of President Franklin Roosevelt's technique of government administration, which deliberately assigned overlapping roles to a multiplicity of agencies and rarely abolished old ones when new ones with similar functions were created. As a means of enhancing FDR's freedom to maneuver, this otherwise bizarre technique had something to commend it. In the international field, however, there is no corresponding chief executive to bring some measure of consistency and common policy direction out of organizational chaos.

Both GATT and UNCTAD are in flux, opening possibilities for change in the established attitudes toward them of various groupings of countries. In its origins, GATT was dominated by industrialized countries, so that both its general rules and the negotiations it supervised were focused on expanded trade among those countries, based on the principles of reciprocity and nondiscrimination. In 1964, however, partly in response to the creation of UNCTAD, a Part IV on trade and development was added to the General Agreement, largely exempting developing countries from obligations of reciprocity. Many of the developing countries actively engaged in world trade have felt it to their advantage to join GATT, so that its present membership is over 80, a large majority coming from the third world. In contrast to IMF and the World Bank, there is no weighted voting; each member casts one vote. As a result, although developing countries continue to regard GATT as mainly an industrialized country organization, and its secretariat is in fact drawn predominantly from OECD countries, there is a strong current of opinion in industrialized countries that GATT has been taken over by developing countries and diverted from its main task of securing freer trade in the industrialized world. For this reason, a special advisory panel of the Atlantic Council of the United States recently has proposed a "GATT Plus," providing for more extensive reciprocal obligations on trade liberalization within an "inner circle" of industrialized countries, with its benefits extended automatically to

developing countries and its membership open to any country prepared to accept the inner circle rules.[14]

UNCTAD, on the other hand, began its life in 1964 as a "ginger
group" for the interests of developing countries in improving their
conditions and terms of trade, their access to international markets,
and the contribution of altered trade policies to their economic
development. The industrialized countries participate in the quad-
rennial conferences and the more frequent meetings of the Trade
and Development Board and its committees, but the secretariat has
been led and dominated by developing country representatives
explicitly devoted to developing country objectives. In fact, UNCTAD
has been a major instrument for reconciling divergent views within
the group of developing countries and bringing about the remarkable
degree of cohesion they have demonstrated in UN and other forums
in recent years. Hence, the traditional attitude of condescension
toward UNCTAD in many industrialized country capitals, regarding
it as a "talk shop" and pressure-venting mechanism for developing
countries, with little impact on actual trading arrangements or
negotiations.

Yet it must be recognized that UNCTAD as a pressure group in
fact has brought about significant changes in the rules of the international economic game. It has secured universal acceptance for
the principles of generalized tariff preferences for developing
country exports and favorable treatment, without reciprocity, in
other aspects of multilateral trade negotiations. It also has contributed substantially to changed attitudes on shipping arrangements,
technology transfer, commodity agreements, and possibly transnational enterprises. In the last few years, just when the rhetorical
temperature was rising in the UN General Assembly, the UNCTAD
secretariat has moved toward a more sober search for reconciliation
of North-South differences and for practical areas of accommodation.
It has sought high professional quality in its staff work, and as a
bureaucratic entity it is clearly anxious to move from a role of
debating and pressure politics into serious negotiation on policies.

If the September 1975 special session of the UN General Assembly really does represent a watershed in North-South relations,
shifting the balance from confrontation to serious negotiation, one
institutional consequence might be an effort to recreate a comprehensive international trade organization (or perhaps an international
trade and development organization) to fill the partial vacuum still
remaining from the nonratification of the Havana Charter of 1948.
A new organization would replace both GATT and UNCTAD, absorb
the ECOSOC Commissions on Natural Resources and Transnational
Corporations, and probably include some kind of coordinating body
for commodity arrangements. The UNCTAD secretariat has given

low-key support to such a reform, and the recent Group of Experts on the Structure of the UN System has endorsed it "as a longer term objective," while stressing that consideration of institutional reform should not interfere with the ongoing Tokyo Round of multinational trade negotiations organized by GATT.

The structure of any newly created entity would certainly be more complex than that envisioned in 1948. It would have to provide separately for debate on principles and for negotiation of binding agreements, but also link them together. It would have to provide explicitly for regional or other groupings of limited membership prepared to assume more far-reaching reciprocal obligations not inconsistent with the global rules. In this category would fit the "GATT Plus" proposal already mentioned in relation to industrialized countries and any corresponding arrangements among groups of developing countries. For the operation of specific commodity arrangements, specialized bodies like the Tin and Wheat Councils would be maintained, informing the new organization of their activities and subject to appropriate general guiding principles. Special rule-making and negotiating procedures would probably be needed for East-West relations. Formal or informal caucuses of like-minded subgroups would obviously not be excluded, whether in the OECD, the Group of 77, or OPEC.

Although the governing assembly of a new international trade organization would doubtless represent all participating countries and adopt the unfortunate but now sacrosanct UN principle of one vote per country, its working organs would have to be much more limited in number and some of them might even experiment with weighted voting. Sponsors of the new Paris Conference on International Economic Cooperation, with its membership of 27 for the coordinating group and 15 each for the functional commissions, have emphasized the critical importance of small numbers in facilitating serious negotiations. The UNCTAD Trade and Development Board, with 68 members, is considered too large, while the executive boards of IMF and the World Bank are "manageable." The same kind of representation devised for CIEC, perhaps with two or three additional seats for Eastern countries, might be applied to the executive council of a new organization.

A new organization could eliminate overlapping data collecting and analytic activities, make more efficient use of scarce staff talent, and provide representational savings to member governments. Such gains, however, might be offset by the costs of a complex institutional negotiation of two or three years' duration. The issue is not so much administrative as political. A well-designed agency could improve the quality of international decision making. Its establishment would symbolize a global consensus among governments that their interests would be served by continuing negotiation of a worldwide framework of rules for trade and related matters conducive to stability and development. In the absence of such a consensus, it would be as well to leave the present disorder unreformed, lest there be destroyed such capacity to promote useful accommodation as present institutions may possess.

The Financial Institutions

A new international trade organization would not have direct access to financial resources. It would have to look to UNDP, IMF, the World Bank, and the regional banks for any needed multilateral public financial support of resource arrangements, whether in the field of supply development, buffer stocks, or compensatory financing. Since there is no realistic prospect of substantial additional voluntary contributions to the UNDP, the focus of attention is on the other named institutions, with the possible addition of new OPEC-financed development banks.

There are noteworthy shifts in attitudes toward the roles and relationships of the Bank and the Fund. Ten or fifteen years ago, the Fund was viewed with deep suspicion by many developing countries, as an institution dominated by conservative industrialized country finance ministries, pressing upon the developing countries excessively orthodox fiscal and monetary policies, and insufficiently interested in their developmental needs. The Bank also was considered too responsive to the industrialized country majority in its weighted voting structure, but it did have development as its main raison d'etre and its resources were eagerly sought. More recently, developing countries have felt the Fund to be more sympathetic to their concerns than in the past, and to contain an important potential for medium and long-term resource transfers as well as shorter term balance-of-payments support. Creation of the compensatory financing facility was an important step in this change, along with more sympathetic consideration of inflationary pressures and support within the Fund's management for a link between the creation of Special Drawing Rights and developing country capital requirements. There is also some indication that, as between the World Bank and the regional banks, developing countries would prefer a larger share of multilateral resource transfer to come through the latter channel because of their control of the governing boards and predominance in the executive staffs.

The net effect of these trends has been an increasing overlap between Fund and Bank responsibilities, visible alike in the emergency efforts to offset the effects of high oil and food prices and in the possible involvement of both institutions in buffer stock financing. Both are involved, and are likely to become more heavily involved, in the sensitive process of discretionary judgment on internal economic policies as conditions of their financial support. At the same time, their boards are increasingly engaged in general policy discussions of topics also under review in the UN economic agencies.

No radical institutional change is likely to develop from these tendencies. Closer policy coordination between the Bank and Fund may be forthcoming through the Joint Ministerial Development Committee established in 1974. Closer staff collaboration, with even more joint studies and joint missions than in the past, are likely to become the order of the day. The developing country pressure for increased voting strength and staff participation may bring about further marginal concessions, as it did in 1975, but can scarcely be pushed to the point of jeopardizing the standing of the Bank in the capital markets of industrialized countries. If an effective international trade organization were to come into being, it might exercise increasing influence on Bank and Fund policies related to trade and development, especially if its policy-making bodies came to include representatives of finance ministries as well as ministries of trade and foreign relations.

An Overall Steering Mechanism?

It is a commonplace to recognize the interdependence of international economic relations in the functional sense, as distinct from the tightening web of activities linking national economies. Thus money and trade, differential rates of inflation, domestic and international capital formation and flows, commodity prices and supplies, cyclical and structural shifts in growth patterns, environmental protection, technological change and its diffusion, and shifts in location of economic activities are all interrelated through complex systems with reciprocal feedbacks. Unregulated market forces bring about continuous adjustments in many of these relationships; others are the object of national governmental intervention; and still others call for international attention to manage crises, to relieve dangerous tensions, or to pursue consensual objectives.

At the operational level, the international economic system must work through a variety of functional agencies of varying geographic scope. Money, trade, and capital transfers cannot be handled in detail by a single institution. Even in the limited field of natural resources, the discussion here suggests that the most streamlined institutional reform would still leave a large number of agencies working in parallel.

The question then arises of whether or not functional interdependence calls for some kind of overall steering body, manageable in size and therefore appointed through some representative process, to provide coherent guidance to the whole family of international economic institutions. Some of the comments surrounding the launching of the new Conference on International Economic Cooperation in Paris suggest that its articulators envision such a role for CIEC. It is significant that the proposal calls for secretariats to be established for each of the four new commissions, at once raising issues of overlap with existing agencies, not only in the financial area but also in the fields of trade, development, and resources.

Without suggesting answers here, it may be useful to pose some questions. Is an overall steering mechanism a desirable or realistic institutional goal? Can it or should it be established independently of the United Nations; if so, will it replace the UN economic structure or compete with it? How will it secure legitimacy in the eyes of nonparticipating governments? In what form will it provide "guidance" to operating agencies and by what means will they be induced to conform to such guidance?

Such questions go well beyond the scope of this paper, but the answers will have a major bearing on the working of the international economic order in the field of natural resources and on even broader issues.

NOTES

1. Donella Meadows et al., The Limits to Growth (New York: Universe Books, 1972).

2. Robert L. Heilbroner, An Inquiry Into the Human Prospect (New York: Norton, 1974).

3. For an exceptionally incisive quantitative analysis of this issue, see Alvin Weinberg and H. E. Goeller, "The Age of Substitutability," Science, February 13, 1976.

4. See H. S. D. Cole et al., Models of Doom: Critique of the Limits to Growth (New York: Universe Books, 1973); G. Carter, "Population, Environment and Natural Resources: A Critical Review of Recent Models," UN, E/Conf. 60/Sym. III/15, August 24, 1973; Wilfred Beckerman, In Defense of Economic Growth (London: Jonathan Cape, 1974), and Wilfred Beckerman's article "Economists, Scientists and Environmental Catastrophe," Oxford Economic Papers, November 1972.

5. Robert L. Heilbroner, "Second Thoughts on The Human Prospect," Challenge, May–June 1975, pp. 21-28.

6. Resources for Freedom, Report by the President's Material Policy Commission (Washington, D.C.: Government Printing Office, 1952).

7. See C. Fred Bergsten, "The Threat from the Third World," Foreign Policy, no. 11, Summer 1973.

8. See Robert V. Ayres and Noble Stedman, "Materials Scarcity and Substitution" (Paper for the Conference Board, International Research and Technology Corporation, Washington, D.C., 1973).

9. International Bank for Reconstruction and Development, Prospects for Exports of Bauxite/Alumina/Aluminum from Developing Countries (Washington, D.C., October 1974).

10. UN, General Assembly Resolution no. 2092, "Permanent Sovereignty Over Natural Resources of Developing Countries and the Expansion of Domestic Sources of Accumulation of Natural Resources for Economic Development," 25th sess., 1970.

11. On GATT, see John Jackson, World Trade and the Laws of GATT (New York: Bobbs-Merrill, 1969); and Kenneth Dam, The GATT: Law—The International Economic Organization (University of Chicago Press, 1970). On UNCTAD, see Branislav Gosovic, UNCTAD, A Political Analysis (New York: William Heinmann, 1968); M. Shah, Developing Countries and UNCTAD (Mystic, Ct.: Verry, Lawrence, 1968); and Diego Cordovez, "UNCTAD and Development Diplomacy: From Compromise to Strategy," Journal of World Trade Law (London), 1971.

12. For an extended discussion of this topic, with specific proposals for GATT revision to deal with it, see C. Fred Bergsten, Completing the GATT: Towards New International Rules to Govern Export Controls (Washington, D.C.: British-North American Committee, 1974).

13. The International Control of Investment: The Dusseldorf Conference on Multinational Corporations (New York: Praeger, 1974), p. 84.

14. See GATT Plus: A Proposal for Trade Reform (Washington, D.C.: Atlantic Council of the United States, 1975, and New York: Praeger, 1976) (the Praeger edition includes the text of the General Agreement).

6

COMMENTS AND
DISCUSSION

INTRODUCTION
Lincoln Gordon

I have circulated a rather long paper. It was suggested to me
by Don Wallace that I make a very brief precis of it before introducing the discussants. My paper is divided into three equal parts,
the first of which summarizes the essential facts on production and
trade in raw materials, excluding oil. It notes the dramatic changes
in control and influence over production and trade in these materials
in recent years. It also seeks to dispel a number of misconceptions
on physical scarcity on the supposed danger of widespread cartels
following the model of the Organization of Petroleum Exporting
Countries (OPEC), and on the typical patterns of industrialized and
developing country interests.

The second section reviews the array of international organizations concerned with natural resources. I have classified them under
four headings, because each of these four fields presents different
kinds of problems. If one were making a completely logical international economic order from scratch, probably each would have its
own set of institutional arrangements. Those four are discovery
and development of resource supplies, conditions of trade, the
international organization of markets, and compensatory financing
for shortfalls in export earnings.

The actual array of institutions is certainly not logical. It is
a somewhat bewildering product of complex political forces and
historic circumstances. There are lots of overlaps and some
important gaps, which are mentioned in the text. I did not think
to use the word "galaxy," which James Grant applied to the food
field. If that is a galaxy, then in the natural resource field, there
must be a whole universe.

The third and concluding section seeks to raise some institutional issues, which I hope will be illuminated by my colleagues on this panel. One has to assume some kind of broad international framework in discussing matters of this kind. My own assumptions include an increasingly interdependent world still governed mainly by sovereign nation-states, with no supranational government. The industrialized and third-world countries are taken to be the main participants in international resource issues, with the role of the second or Communist world being significant but marginal. On the West-South axis, which is the major focus, I assume that relations will continue as an uneasy mixture of confrontation and somewhat suspicious collaboration, but that the confrontational element will diminish in relation to practical efforts to find common meeting grounds of mutual interest, looking toward accelerated development of the South, but without a major transfer of basic wealth or income, as distinct from incremental income, from the West.

Within that framework, four issues are suggested for discussion. The first is how to develop stable and acceptable arrangements for mineral discovery and development, including the financing of the inevitable dry holes. I am dubious about investment codes for that purpose, but rather hopeful about new kinds of negotiations between mining companies and host governments, with encouragement from international financial institutions. Out of that process, there might gradually evolve a kind of case law for eventual codification.

At the conference that Don Wallace presided over at Dusseldorf in 1973, I made a similar suggestion. It was then treated quite cursorily by the representative of the legal department of the World Bank, but two years later it now seems to be gaining wide acceptance.

The second issue arises from the large overlap between UNCTAD (United Nations Conference on Trade and Development) and GATT (General Agreement on Tariffs and Trade), which is the most striking institutional anomaly in this general resource field. Both are in a rather fluid institutional and political condition, a fact that makes timely a reopening of the question of the utility of an international trade organization that would replace both. Today, such an organization would obviously have to be a more complex organization than the one negotiated in the Havana Charter in 1948.

A related issue of potentially large importance concerns the new Paris Conference on International Economic Cooperation (CIEC), which is expected to create a new set of commissions in the four fields of energy, natural resources, development, and financing. Will CIEC simply replace duplication by triplication?

The third issue is related to Henry Costanzo's role. It has to do with the shifting activities in the resource field of the various

financial institutions—the International Monetary Fund, the World
Bank, the International Finance Corporation (IFC), the UN Development Program, and the regional banks—together with possible
changes in government attitudes toward those institutions. There
seems to be an increasing interpenetration of activities, especially
between the Fund and the Bank, which may raise some difficult
problems in coming years. Obviously, the creation of the Joint
Development Committee was a reflection, in part, of that interpenetration.

Finally, the fourth point is a very broad one, related to the
issue of functional interdependence among the many elements of the
international economic order. It concerns the possible need for
some kind of overall steering mechanism—something which would
be representative in character, but more manageable in size and
more realistic in approach than the Economic and Social Council
of the UN, which, according to the Charter, has that kind of responsibility. Is such a mechanism desirable? Is it practicable? If it
were created, how would it relate to other institutions and what
would connect the steering wheel with the operating parts?

Now, with that brief summary, I would like to present our
panelists. The order stated on the program is alphabetical—
Armstrong, Bergsten, and Pollock—and we will proceed in that
order. All are old personal friends.

Willis Armstrong is a consultant to the U.S. Council of the International Chamber of Commerce. He has had a distinguished government, academic, and business career, including many positions in
the Foreign Service, abroad and at home. In very recent years,
he served as assistant secretary of state for economic affairs from
1972 to 1974.

Our second panelist is Fred Bergsten, a senior fellow of the
Brookings Institution. Fred is so well known in person and from
his writings that he certainly does not require further introduction.
In addition to his really great distinction as a scholar in this field
of applied international economics, he has had considerable responsibility in government posts, first in the Department of State in the
mid-1960s and then on the White House staff with the National
Security Council in the period 1969-71.

Our third panelist is David Pollock. David is a Canadian
citizen who has played a very quiet but influential role on the international economic scene. It flows from his very long association
with Raul Prebisch first in Chile in the Economic Commission for
Latin America (ECLA), then in the formative stage of UNCTAD and
during the years that Dr. Prebisch was secretary general, and here
in recent years as director of ECLA, Washington Office.

COMMENT
Willis Armstrong

Lincoln Gordon's is an absolutely first-class survey of the facts in the situation, an excellent picture of the landscape. It indicates where all the main features are and it raises fundamental questions about the relationships between these various features of the landscape and about where we are going in the field of what might be called "global resource management."

There has been, of course, very little global management, which does not mean, however, that there are not a lot of organizations that would be glad to do the managing if somebody would give them a chance.

I think, again, as my question to Edwin Martin implied, here we need to get our eye on the capacity or capability for growth, because with a world population that is going to double by the end of the century, we are going to have more demands for material things. Material things take resources, particularly natural resources of metals and fibers.

Until now, the supply of mineral and fiber resources has been pretty good. I had a certain amount of experience with rubber about 20 years ago. As we all know, in wartime, we were cut off from certain supplies of natural rubber. Therefore, the synthetic industry developed. This is a very fortunate thing, because the world supply of rubber now is about three quarters or two thirds synthetic and about one third natural. If it had not been for the synthetic, there would not have been enough rubber to go around, because the places where rubber grows and the conditions under which it can grow profitably are not all that numerous.

In general, the question of supply, however, is now clouded very badly by the problem of investment incentives. The chairman of a large American mining company, with a big international array of activities, said in my hearing the other day that under no circumstances would he consider using any of his money or his company's money to invest in any developing country in the future for resources. He said he would be perfectly happy to make available the skills of his company in using somebody else's money for such development. But put their own money at risk?—not at all. They are going into coal mining in the United States.

The incentives to invest for mining companies are very seriously impaired, just as they are impaired for oil companies. If you are going to have your supply grow, you need capital. I do not know if the statistics would support this, but one gets the impression that the world is spending capital faster than it is accumulating it. The supply of capital needed for new industrial material development is colossal. Just as it is for new energy development.

There is a tendency, as one moves into an era where national sovereignties are engaged in programs of national socialism, to think that capital can be created by printing money. And, with over 100 sovereignties in the world and every one with a printing press, the capacity is impressive. Therefore, I think the fundamental questions raised and those that need a great deal of emphasis are where is the capital going to come from for the investment and under what circumstances is it to be made available?

There has been a shift pursuant to the suggestions made by the Kissinger-Moynihan speech on September 1 into the area of encouraging capital investment by the World Bank or the International Monetary Fund in resource development. This is the natural reaction to the political facts of life among large numbers of the developing countries, which have managed to drive or scare away private development capital. This probably has some promising possibilities, because mining companies have skills, knowledge, talents, and marketing mechanisms, and can be persuaded to go in on a fee or an agency or a marketing or technical advisory capacity to work with nationalized enterprises. They are probably prepared to do so.

But if the capital is going to be raised by the World Bank, we should not overlook the fact that the World Bank depends essentially on the world financial market as a means of raising capital, certainly for enterprises that are supposed to be profit making and that presumably ought to be. The availability of capital to the World Bank is also a factor in considering what kind of change one has to think about in getting away from the decline of private enterprise in extractive work in the developing countries.

In terms of the basic supply of commodities, there are consolations. One is that by no means are all the materials needed for world industry in developing countries. A great many of them are in developed countries, as Gordon pointed out.

Also, there is, presumably, a large supply of such commodities in the Communist countries. At the moment, Poland is raising money to invest in copper and coal, and a fair amount of Polish copper and coal is coming into the world markets. The Soviet Union undoubtedly has masses of material that it could sell if it chose to develop them. I think I am slightly encouraged by the fact that the USSR has drawn closer to the outside world in its international economic activities in the past two or three years. It has expensive appetites and it may just decide something other than gold could be dug out of the ground and made available.

When I was with Peter Peterson, secretary of commerce in 1972, in Russia, we tackled the Russians on platinum and said that we had discovered that we needed platinum for auto emission devices. They said, "oh, well, you know, that's a strategic material." And the conversation did not progress much beyond that. And I do not think that they believed that we thought that it was necessary for the emission devices.

Now, I would like to move on for a minute to comment on the question of commodity stabilization. Certainly there is a case for trying to ease the fluctuations in commodity markets. The case has been made many times. Some years ago I spent a lot of time working on the commodity problems in the State Department. The experience left me with some very strong convictions. One is that there is very little that a collection of governments can do to affect substantively market trends in commodities. That does not mean that they will not try. They will try. The argument is logical. If you have stable conditions, you will encourage production. And it will be there when consumption increases. Therefore, people talk about buffer stocks and that sort of thing.

I do think that it is the wrong place on which to put major emphasis. The major emphasis should be on conditions under which the supply of goods for the world market can be increased and on the maintenance of some kind of a market mechanism that will enable people who have goods to sell them efficiently to people who need them.

Lincoln Gordon's comment on international organizations is very well taken. I did detect, while I was in the Department of State, and since I have left, a very strong distaste on the part of Henry Kissinger for any existing international institutions. He also has a strong inclination to take the initiative in starting something new, which might not have had a strictly bureaucratic objective but certainly did have an objective of appearing to strike out into bold new fields. Therefore, one can only wait and see what happens with this new Conference on International Economic Cooperation (CIEC) in Paris. We experimented in 1950, 1951, and 1952 with a temporary organization in commodities, called the International Materials Conference. It was designed to be temporary and we made sure it was, and abolished it when the crisis was over.

In general, in this area, I am fairly gloomy. I am not against international organizations, but I do not think they amount to much in terms of affecting the production, sales, distribution, and consumption of goods. I think the effort at stabilization is in the distributive area. And under conditions of a philosophical sort of approach that involves some amount of socialist doctrine, there is always more interest in distribution than there is in production among socialists and those who stress social rather than economic values.

As we go into the future, fundamental economic forces will tend to continue to govern. People will not buy goods they do not need. The pressure of OPEC (Organization of Petroleum Exporting Countries) on oil prices, in combination with inflation and the general uncertainty prevalent in the world, probably will limit the effectiveness of demand for basic commodities. Therefore, I would be surprised if we had any near term boom of the 1972-73 proportions that hit all the basic raw materials alike.

I expect that all nation-states will expand their control over their own resources and seek to get a little more control over other people's resources. This departure, generally, from the market mechanism will probably result in a slowdown in production and an increase in costs, coming at a time when there ought to be an expansion of production and a reduction of costs so that people's needs will be met. Therefore, the actions of governments will have the opposite effects of what they say they shall. But I think that is the way it will happen. I do not see any real prospects for gains in real income by the producers of basic commodities—or, for that matter, by the consumers—simply because of the uncertainty of general market conditions and the unlikelihood that stabilization measures will amount to much. I would, therefore, expect that everybody's frustrations will increase and political disarray will spread. And the requirements of industry for the world's population will not be met as satisfactorily as they might otherwise.

To some extent, I think this is in large part a result of the decline of the use of the market mechanism or of extensive and unwarranted interference with it, all with perfectly laudable social and national objectives. Again, I say national socialism. I know it was a discredited term in the 1930s, but it still is an accurate description.

I would expect the United States to be able to take care of itself pretty well under these circumstances, and I would expect it to be a little rougher with some other people than it might have been in the past. Despite the responsive line taken in the speech of September 1, I do not really agree with James Grant that this was a major change in policy. Rather, I think it was a recognition, an awareness, of the political forces in the world that were demanding a change. It was a responsiveness in general, but with action or specifics reserved for the future. I am not at all sure that this is going to result in any specific responsiveness over time. I am not even suggesting necessarily that it should, because many things that are demanded would be counter to U.S. economic interests. But we may well get to a stage in a couple of years where people in developing countries would feel extremely disturbed that they had not seen the results that they thought they were going to get on the basis of the rhetoric of September. This is politically, of course, an unfortunate prospect. I am not suggesting that one should not have been responsive. I am simply saying that the form of responsiveness resulted in the rather chaotic language that one finds in the resolution of the Seventh Special Session—which I defy anybody really to explain clearly. Thus far, of course, international organizations have dealt only in rhetoric and that is their normal stock in trade.

The problem, as I see it, is a need for the production of goods and services, and not the production of rhetoric. And, on the institutional side, I think everybody has recognized that world interdependence is here—and is necessary and inevitable. But nobody is ready to act on this basis. Therefore, when one talks in terms of the capacity of the world to have any sort of overall guidance or operation—shall we say command post or general staff—this is highly unlikely, because it is beyond the realm of human capability. By now, most countries have got life so complicated for themselves that they cannot manage their own affairs. And, therefore, I do not see any particular reason to think that anybody could manage a world economy.

COMMENT
Fred Bergsten

I would like to make some comments, first on the analytic part of Lincoln Gordon's paper. Then I would like to devote more attention to the policy proposals where, despite agreeing with Willis Armstrong that nobody can run the world nor should be put in a position to do so, I think I would go a bit farther than Gordon indicates in trying to generate some institutional changes, to deal with the various aspects of the problem that his paper points out.

There are a number of things in the analysis of the paper that I fully agree with, for example, that there is no threat of physical shortages and the fact that political issues are as important as economic issues in this whole area. Indeed, it is the political issues that both Gordon and Armstrong have mentioned that have cut the supply elasticity so sharply in this area.

Cartels, commodity prices—prices that have been high—historically always have been broken from the supply side, not the demand side. And political factors, as both noted, have really cut very sharply into the elasticity of supply response. And that is one of the major problems as I see it and will elaborate on.

I also fully agree that the basic factors of the issue are the West and the South. There will be a mix of confrontation and collaboration. I think that is a fascinating issue right now for the South. It has gotten where it got in terms of turning U.S. policy around to some extent and getting people's attention through confrontation. But now, obviously, it wants, at least a bit, to try to strengthen the hands of those who want to collaborate with it. Therefore, it has got to find a delicate balance between the confrontation and collaboration now, which is a tougher job, than the straightforward confrontation route that provided cement for the Group of 77 and made its job relatively easy as long as the United States was stonewalling anything as recently as April and breaking up the first prepcon in Paris.

There are a couple of other analytic points in Gordon's paper with which I am less in agreement. It is quite true, factually, that the industrial countries are the main sources of commodity output, aggregating everything together. But I think that is a misleading statement for a couple of reasons. One is that I regard Canada and Australia, which are, as noted, big elements in the production of many raw materials, as not really part of the industrialized, consuming world for these purposes. They view themselves with the producers. They are joining all of the producer's associations. They have stonewalled in the OECD and in other forums any efforts to write new rules of the game that would help consumer interests. And therefore I do not regard them as part of the industrial world, as one normally thinks of it for these purposes.

In addition, the developing countries are the dominant suppliers of a number of important primary products, both minerals and foodstuffs. And therefore the North-South politicization angle plays a bigger role in the issue than one might infer from just the aggregate data that the developed countries are suppliers of more than half of the world's raw materials.

The main concern I have about the analytic part of the paper is that it leaves me hanging and wondering if there is a problem—and if so, what it is. I think Gordon has presented the situation very nicely, but there really was not a bottom line in the sense of saying, "Is there a problem? If so, what is it?" I think there is a problem. And I am looking at it mainly from the standpoint of a consuming or importing country—the United States—but also Western Europe and Japan.

What impresses me about the commodity markets right now is how strong they are. Now, in the depth of by far the deepest recession in the postwar period, commodity prices have remained much higher than anybody would have thought to be the case, running any kind of correlations with the previous aggregate demand pictures. The commodity prices turned down much later in the cycle than they ever had before. Indeed, they lagged by a couple of quarters instead of leading by a couple of quarters as they traditionally had. In fact, they have already turned up much earlier in the upswing than would have been anticipated. So on a variety of criteria I am impressed and worried by the fact, from the standpoint of a consumer, that the commodity markets are just very strong.

The second problem is that they are very unstable. Everybody is agreed to that. A third and underlying factor, which I have already mentioned briefly, is that both the demand and the supply elasticities really have declined very sharply and, therefore, have made us much less able to rely on the market mechanisms than we could in the past.

There are a lot of structural changes on both the demand and particularly the supply sides of the markets in most of these raw materials that make it just less likely—much less likely than in the past—that we will get any kind of quick response through market factors to deal with the commodity price and instability problems.

Then, finally, and buttressed by the first three concerns, is my difference with Gordon, which is well known and recorded throughout the literature, on the likelihood of contrived shortages, of which there are now at least ten producer associations by a conservative count functioning to push their returns up even higher, particularly in a strong market. But I certainly do not rule out the possibility that some of them, as they have, can act very effectively even in a weak market.

I think there is a problem along those four lines and that leads me to take a more activist position and to try to do something more about it than is suggested in Gordon's paper. The first policy area that he addressed was the need for increased production in a number of commodity areas. Armstrong agreed with that view and I certainly agree with that very, very strongly. But I think more is needed than what Gordon called for: a new framework for negotiations between the firms and the host governments or simply paying homage to the market, hoping that somehow it will get back into the picture more broadly. I really think we need some structural changes in the way in which the multinational firms relate to the host country governments. It essentially boils down to their getting out of equity.

Armstrong has already testified that the firms do not want to put in any equity capital, and I think that is a constructive step in the right direction. Because only to the extent that they are willing to move in on a nonequity basis are we likely to restore any degree of stability to the relationship between investors and host country governments and, therefore, get any chance of bringing the supply elasticity up to where it has been historically.

Incidentally, I think that is probably a very good deal for the firms. A number of firms already have begun to go the management contract route, are very pleased with it, and regard their contracts as very lucrative and certainly much less risky than in the past.

What is needed here also is to try to multinationalize the investment process as much as possible—not only to get out of equity but also to try to hook in a lot of different financiers for the project through the debt market. Maybe the way is to sell forward the output to consumers in a lot of industrial-using companies—Germany, Japan, the United States, and elsewhere—and try to get as many eggs in the basket in terms of companies and nationalities as possible. Then, if the host country decides it wants to rewrite the rules of the game later on, it will be taking on a whole lot of people. It is very easy, really, for Chile to sock it to U.S. firms because it has Japanese and Europeans standing in the wake. But if a lot of people are hooked into the game, then it is much more difficult.

I would try to push all this through the Overseas Private Investment Corporation (OPIC), especially to push the multinationals into raw materials investment on a nonequity basis. OPIC, quite logically, has gotten out of the raw materials business the last few years because of the obvious risk of ensuring equity in that sector. I think it ought to get back into the area in a big way but push nonequity processes. In fact, it is doing that with an oil investment in the Philippines. Furthermore, OPIC in the United States should try to collaborate with its 16 counterparts in the other industrial countries to try to get them jointly to promote this kind of financing for investment in the developing countries. The OPICs already do collaborate on a variety of issues, and this kind of collaboration would be very helpful in getting at the supply side that Gordon quite rightly points to in his paper and Armstrong refers to as an important area.

There is another international kind of convention that I would advocate in trying to improve this process, what is sometimes called in the jargon a "hot products convention," an agreement among the industrial countries that are the main importers of these raw materials to permit firms to sue in each other's courts to tie up hot products, so that when the host countries—if they do tear up the rules, expropriate, and so on—go back on agreements that are made, there is legal redress that can rebound unfavorably to the interests of the host country.

The industrial countries have a joint interest in this area. They have recognized it in oil in the IEA. The United States and the other consuming countries should be making much more explicit and aggressive efforts to pool their interests to boost the level, diversity, and stability of output.

The second area that Gordon raised was the conditions of trade. He mentioned, but did not advocate, new rules to govern access to supplies in the traditional trade sense, analogous to the rules that have existed for a generation governing access to markets. This is a critical element in the whole picture. It clearly is not negotiable just by itself. But as part of a package of arrangements that met the legitimate interest and demands of the producing countries, it seems both feasible and extremely valuable.

The GATT rules have not been perfect. We have had import controls put on from time to time, but it has been a world apart from the 1930s, and has, on the whole, worked very well. It has been protection against protectionism. In the access to supply area, new international rules, which I would put in GATT, to govern access to supplies and limit recourse to export controls, the same way we have limited recourse to import controls, would be very desirable.

Here, I must say I take issue with my friend David Pollock. I do not agree with his basic point that the postwar international economic system helped the big guys but not the little guys. The growth record of the developing countries in the postwar period is unprecedented in history. Their exports of manufactures increased at rates undreamed of 15 years ago. The system has helped them very greatly. Maybe it could have done more, but it certainly helped them very greatly.

In this area, there has been tremendous asymmetry. There have been rules that gave them access to markets under a lot of conditions that made it hard for importing countries to mess things up. But there really have not been any rules to limit their recourse to export controls or other limitations to their export of supplies, as we have seen very clearly in the last two or three years.

In the area of commodity organization, I believe that there is a place for a number of commodity agreements. I take that position not just from the standpoint of producers trying to stabilize their returns, but even more so from the standpoint of importing countries, as consumers, trying to put limits on the price to which imports go. We should put floor prices under the markets to maintain the flow of investment, which is much discouraged when prices collapse, as is done in short-run periods even after they have gone to astronomical highs and remain high in historic terms. From the economic standpoint of the importing countries, including the United States, commodity agreements are desirable.

Institutionally, I would do them ad hoc, a la tin, coffee, and others. There have been proposals for an overarching commodity code with a lot of principles and all that. I do not see too much objection to it, though it might waste some time in getting into the specifics. On this one point, however, I would support the U.S. official position of doing it case by case. But I would hope that would lead to actually doing it case by case, rather than rejecting it case by case as had been true in the past.

In the final substantive area, finance, it is probably desirable to liberalize the compensatory finance facility at the IMF as proposed in the Kissinger speech to the UN. But it has to be remembered that compensatory finance only involves loans, maybe some grants for the poorest groups but largely loans. It therefore is not going to be viewed by the producers as a substitute for price stabilization. Since that is true, it probably would not stabilize the investment and production process that I think is important to the United States and other countries as consumers. Indeed, I would see commodity agreements and income stabilization agreements as complements, each targeted on different objectives, rather than having different or substitutional roles to play.

Finally, Gordon raised the idea of an international trade organization, which he put a bit differently, from the original International Trade Organization. His organization seems to be an amalgam only of GATT and UNCTAD. The original organization, of course, went much farther and had chapters on commodities and investment and labor standards—practically everything that came under the ruberic of international economics. I would certainly oppose this original concept at this point in time. What we have learned is that the institutions that work are those that are functionally specific—be it IMF, GATT, or OPEC whose results I do not like—the ones that have worked have been functionally specific and did not get into ancillary issues. I do not like big, general, multipurpose organizations. They demonstrably do not work in achieving objective tasks. They may provide useful forums for discussion, consultation, and rhetoric. I do not object to that, but we should not be misled that there is going to be real action in those kinds of institutions.

Maintaining both GATT and UNCTAD does not bother me either. I do not think it bothers most of the developing countries, frankly. I observe a number of them being very serious about GATT negotiations and the Multilateral Trade Negotiations. They know that is where the action is. They know that is where the money is to be made. They are taking it very seriously, even when they are not GATT members. I do not mind the continued GATT institution doing the real business on trade negotiations, with UNCTAD being more the pressure group for the developing countries and a place where studies can be done and rhetoric let off—a function I would hope to keep there, rather than rolling into GATT, which is always a risk if the two institutions are fused.

If you do not fuse, and if you do not set up an international trade organization, you face the question that Gordon raises, quite rightly: How do you coordinate things? My own answer is that you have to do it very informally. There is no legitimate coordinating mechanism. Coordination has to be done by the few biggest guys, quietly, in a

smoke-filled room. None of us pay much homage to that, because
we know it does not carry much of an aura of legitimacy. But we
know, in fact, it has to be done. That does not answer the question
as to who is in that room and who is doing it. In my view, it has
got to include representatives not just of the rich industrial countries
of the past but of the nouveau riche and OPEC and some of the most
important developing countries.

Therefore, the new CIEC may have some merit. But, again,
I think it is probably already overly institutionalized with 27 members,
probably already too big to play the kind of role of this type. I would
suspect that the coordination is going to have to be worked out through
small informal groups of one or two people from six to eight countries, meeting in a chateau on the Loire, as they have done in the
monetary field in the last couple of years. But it must be broadened
to cover this whole range of economic issues and then continue to
implement through the functionally specific existing international
economic institutions, with one or two added on, such as I have
suggested.

COMMENT
David Pollock

At the very outset, I would like to make two comments that are
somewhat personal in nature. One is that originally I had intended
to speak from a formal written statement that I had prepared awhile
back. Just five minutes ago, however, I decided to put that statement aside and speak extemporaneously. This was mainly because
the comments of Fred Bergsten and Willis Armstrong, together
with Lincoln Gordon's paper, have covered the details of the topic
in such a comprehensive way that I really would now prefer not
more point-by-point coverage but rather to try my hand at something a bit more general and less formal than I had originally
prepared. The second is that, although I am a Canadian and
stationed in Washington, my work basically involves development
issues as seen from the developing countries' point of view. So
I would like to act as sort of a devil's advocate here, in this room
full of powerful voices, from powerful U.S. private and public
agencies, since I am the only non-U.S. speaker on the entire roster.
Therefore, if you will excuse me for speaking rather more broadly
and bluntly than I had first intended to do, and bearing in mind the
very brief time available to me, I would like to try and sketch out,
in a somewhat philosophic vein, the case for a new way of thinking
about the words "international economic order" that appeared in
the title of Gordon's paper. And then I would like to consider the

role of commodity policy (or resource policy, as it is being called here today) as an essential element in that new order of things.

Someone, I think it was Fred Bergsten, began by saying that Gordon's paper left him hanging in the sense that it didn't indicate clearly whether or not there is a problem and, if so, what it is. I had the same reaction since the paper implied that there is, in fact, no need for a new global commodity policy for development nor for related institutional machinery in the international commodity field. I do not agree with this, and I will tell you why I feel this way.

Rightly or wrongly, the developing countries' perception of international trade theory and the policy implications flowing from that theory diverge sharply from the classic approaches, which are those still largely held here. The developing countries believe that, when foreign trade takes place without impediment, and under conditions of comparative advantage, it does not do what it professes to do, namely, maximize global welfare all around. On the contrary, they view it as having served historically as an instrumentality of economic disadvantage, of contributing to a skewed pattern of global income and wealth.

My point isn't to try and justify this perception, although I think a strong case could be made for it. But, I can assure you, this is how developing countries view the classic theory of international trade and its impact on nations. Their view has its fundamental origin, as I said, in the concepts of comparative cost and comparative advantage, namely, what happens to the distribution of global income when developing countries mainly export primary products (the prices of which they historically could not control) and import manufactures (the prices of which are largely controlled in developed countries). There is the crux of the matter.

I would like to bring to your attention Lord Keynes' very prescient memorandum that he sent to the U.K. Treasury in 1942 in order to recommend, well before Bretton Woods, that three basic international institutions be set up after World War II. One was to be an International Economic Committee, designed to make official long-term development loans for reconstruction and development. This subsequently became the World Bank. Second, Keynes suggested the creation of an International Clearing Union to facilitate appropriate exchange rate and short-term balance-of-payments adjustments. This subsequently became the International Monetary Fund. But he also urged the creation of a third international institution, namely, a General Council for Commodity Controls. For reasons still unclear to me, the latter not only did not surface at Bretton Woods but indeed was never heard about again, at least not in the developed countries. If you are interested in all this, Keynes 1942 memorandum had been treated as a classified item for many years, but it is now in the public domain.

I wonder if you gentlemen, so knowledgeable on the realities of U.S. needs, interests, and power, can grasp this perception by developing countries of the rules of the game concerning international trade? How, in the face of the literally explosive postwar growth rate in world trade, those rules of the game lead to a very asymetrical diffusion of the fruits of such growth? It is a fact that developing countries' share of world exports (excluding petroleum) has fallen steadily from about 28 percent in 1950 to less than 15 percent today. Do you think, as so many in the developed world do, that this is due basically to internal policy deficiencies on the part of the developing countries? Or do you think, as I do, that it is due fundamentally to structural factors, such as I have mentioned, that are largely beyond developing countries' control? Rightly or wrongly, this perception of global inequities, resulting from international trade theory and practice, has contributed to a very powerful sense of global frustration on the part of the developing world. So I would like to suggest to you that the central problem of our panel (which I thought Gordon's paper was going to present, but which was only partly covered) still needs to be debated; namely, what are some essential elements of an international commodity policy that could reduce or eliminate such inequities?

Well, bearing in mind my time constraint, I would like to list three central elements of such a policy. One is that there should be access to supplies at reasonable prices from the consumers' point of view. Second, there should be access to markets at a remunerative price to producers. But third, and of great importance, as has been stressed repeatedly in the writings of Prebisch and many others in the third world, there must—and I emphasize this—there must be a greater degree of short-term stability in export revenues and long-term equity in the terms of trade of commodities of export interest to developing countries. I am presenting things in a simplified manner in order to save time. But the latter points of emphasis are so important that they bear repeating. Stability of commodity export prices and especially of export revenues in the short-term and appropriate means of adjustment for changes in commodity terms of trade in the long-run are imperatives in any new international policy for development—hence, the close linkage between commodity policy and development policy.

Let us look for a moment at these two short- and long-term issues. I think Secretary of State Henry Kissinger's proposal for a new development security facility, which he presented at the Seventh Special Session of the UN General Assembly two months ago, is an excellent initiative. In essence, it proposes to expand significantly the volume and simultaneously ease the terms and conditions of the existing IMF Compensatory Financing Facility.

Fine. That could help substantially in bringing about short-term
stability in export revenues. That's fine. But as you all know,
and as both Gordon and Bergsten stressed, a compensatory financing
facility can only stabilize an export revenue trend. It cannot raise
it. So, if in addition to accepting the case for short-term revenue
stabilization, you also accept the case for some kind of terms of
trade adjustment—and this case, in my view, will inexorably be
made—then you also have to accept some new approaches to the
organization of commodity markets.

I can understand what Willis Armstrong is trying to say, and
I know his viewpoint is widespread here. But I also feel that somebody in this colloquium should try, on grounds of "equal time," also
to present the viewpoint of developing countries: namely, if you
don't intervene in the marketplace, whether commodity-by-commodity
or on a multicommodity integrated basis, then you simply cannot
change the long-term trend. So, in the short-term, by all means
let's push forward on Secretary Kissinger's development security
facility. But I would be even more sympathetic to that particular
idea if it could also allow, over the long-run, for some adjustments
in import prices as well as in export prices, and not just in the
latter alone. A few moments before our colloquium began, I was
told that something along those lines is being considered right now
within IMF. I hope that is true, since it would be an excellent
addition to the secretary's initiative.

In this same context I was struck by Luis Escobar's remark
that existing international lending organizations must rethink their
policies of the last 25 years. He said, in essence, that the World
Bank and the regional development banks should be thinking along
some fundamentally new lines of endeavor: endeavors that would
lead to additionality in lending volume over and above that which
will result from their traditional types of project financing. This
strikes me as an admirable suggestion. Based on the same type of
reasoning, I, too, ask why, when discussing international commodity
policy, one cannot conceive of some fundamentally new ideas pertaining to commodity market organization. More specifically, one
should be able to consider some type of direct intervention into
commodity markets as a new approach to international development
policy without this being linked, with unhappy semantic connotations,
to "national socialism" or other such geopolitical terms.

I would like to close my remarks by suggesting the need for a
more flexible conceptual approach to an international commodity
policy. There is, I believe, much merit in considering the original
Keynesian proposal for a separate general commodity council.
There is also much need to expand the IMF Compensatory Financing
Facility, as recently recommended by Secretary Kissinger. And I

don't believe those ideas require new institutional machinery. On the contrary, IMF, IBRD, and UNCTAD could and should be used more in the commodity field.

A few words about UNCTAD. Ever since the first UNCTAD conference was held in Geneva during 1964, there has been very strong opposition to UNCTAD concepts and recommendations within the developed world, and certainly within this city. Yet I would like to pose a paradoxical thought. Make a list, heading by heading of the contents of the so-called "Consensus Resolution" that resulted from the Seventh UN Special Session. Then compare that list with the contents, paragraph by paragraph, of Secretary Kissinger's speech at that same UN session. Then, finally, compare each of the latter with the recommendations that emanated from UNCTAD I and II. You will find, probably to your surprise, that they are all virtually mirror images of one another. That is to say, Secretary Kissinger's famous "41 points," the Consensus Resolution that was adopted unanimously by developed as well as developing countries, and the prior UNCTAD recommendations, are all more or less identical. And they all had their origin in the UN development system. Thus, today, UNCTAD can at last be seen for what it is: a moderate and developmentally oriented entity. It is forum for technical advances on economic growth policies, and not a forum for political confrontation, as has so often been presented in Washington. I have long hoped, as I think James Grant and Edwin Martin said earlier, that if the next decade is to be one of negotiation rather than confrontation, it will finally be seen that UNCTAD's main role is not to provoke the developed world for mischievous ends but rather to get it to pay attention to some new thoughts about a changing international economic order.

If, therefore, we all want the next decade to be one of negotiations and commitments, in comparison with the last decade of ideology and confrontation, then paradoxically the developed countries may find to their surprise that there is much they can support in UNCTAD's recommendations. There is much in those recommendations that would be of mutual benefit and advantage to both the developed and the developing world. But UNCTAD needs to be strengthened by some indication of support from the developed countries. If this could be done, you would find it a useful negotiating forum, with virtually global coverage. This would not require the creation of any new machinery but simply the strengthening of an existing one, and, to repeat, offering mutual advantages to developed and developing countries alike.

So I close as I began, on a personal note. I urge you to consider, not as a radical thought but rather as a suggestion from a moderate in Washington, that developed countries contemplate the strategy of giving some greater support to UNCTAD. It already has the support of the developing world. It could, if appropriately strengthened, comprise an existing instrumentality for new approaches to international commodity policy and thereby to international development policy—an instrumentality that is ready, willing, and, I am convinced, able.

DISCUSSION

Lincoln Gordon

Let me raise one point with Fred Bergsten. On the question of changing the GATT rules for access to supplies, my paper apparently did not make clear that my reference to his pamphlet in a footnote was meant to indicate full support. A second point I would like to raise goes back to the matter of resource production and Bergsten's suggestions about the mining companies being pushed unilaterally into nonequity positions. He speaks of their satisfaction with management contracts, presumably of the fixed fee variety.

Two problems trouble me. One is how do the dry holes get financed. That requires risk capital. There is a large risk-bearing function that somebody has to perform and somebody has to finance. The major stage of discovery of minerals, which is between the geological survey phase and the actual mining, seems to be getting increasingly expensive, in spite of important technological improvements ranging from earth resource satellites to learning about the mineral content of the subsoil from the content of the bark on the trees. I do not see in the structure that Bergsten recommends an answer to that problem.

The second problem concerns incentives to effective performance. I do not think it can be answered simply by shifting from equity to debt. It is highly desirable that there be some incentives, which fixed fees do not provide. There can be sliding scale fees of one kind or another. There are ways of participating in the gains from higher productivity output of the mining enterprise, other than the traditional one of equity participation. Our contacts with companies in this business may differ, but my own impression is that, without some kind of incentive reward structure, the chances of getting fully satisfactory performance are not very good.

Perhaps, like Willis Armstrong, I have an old-fashioned belief in the power of economic motivations. But, it does seem to me, that it makes a difference and one should not rule out the elements of risk bearing, incentives, and profit.

Fred Bergsten

I agree that there is no single formula that is going to characterize all of these arrangements between multinationals and host country
governments. I do think, though, that they are going to have to come
within the broad context of, at most, minority equity participation,
and probably nonequity, of a variety of sorts that are mentioned.
Sliding scale incentives to the productivity of the exploration or
marketing that the companies are doing are clearly possible. But
the basic point is that the continued desire of some, though a
diminishing number, companies to continue to go in and own subsoil
rights is just going to turn the whole process off and therefore be
disadvantageous to all parties involved.

Gordon asks where the capital is going to come from. I think
that increasingly the dry hole problem will be financed by the host
country governments themselves. That cost is not as great as the
term "dry holes" implies, because, although one has to drill for
oil, one would have a much better knowledge of whether or not
copper or tin is there. So the relative cost of exploration is not as
high as the oil companies have in that particular industry.

The capital can come from the host country governments
themselves. It can come from people putting up what amounts to
debt capital, but with a higher return than one would normally get
on debt capital because the risk is higher. I think there are a
variety of possibilities. The main point is to do it on a structural
basis that is more stable.

Edwin M. Martin

I would like to address a question to Fred Bergsten. I think
the question of access to supply is a very important one. But it
was being talked about somewhat more actively, at least by the
U.S. government, a year ago or so than it is currently. In this
connection, it did come up in some of the preparations for the
World Food Conference.

It becomes quite clear that negotiation on this cannot be confined
to just natural resources; food is apt to be brought into the picture.
And the minute food is brought into the picture, other factors than
trade controls are highlighted, namely, production controls, which
could also be important with respect to other raw materials. There
can be no limitations on the export of grains, but if farmers are told
not to produce more than 70 percent of what they can, it amounts to
the same thing. I would suspect that the evasion of a trade arrangement will take place in other commodities. I wonder what your view
on this particular question is.

Fred Bergsten

The reason that people were more interested a year ago in access to supply was because that is when the commodity price boom was topping off. It was uppermost in everybody's mind. Immediately upon the decline to prices that are still way above historic levels, but nevertheless down from the highs of the recent past, people concluded that the problem would go away. Some people conjured up analogies to the aftermath of the Korean War. We do not, of course, know yet.

I have argued—this was part of the debate—that the high prices are going to come back pretty soon and pretty savagely. If that happens, people again will be worried about access to supply rules.

Martin is certainly right that it would have to include food as well as raw materials. I view that as desirable. International rules that would put some limits on U.S. ability to slap export controls on soybeans or wheat are every bit as desirable as international rules that would slap limits on what the Jamaicans can do on bauxite or the Saudis on oil. Martin is also quite right in saying that is not just export controls; that is domestic production controls. We all know that is the toughest area to deal with. But the analogy with the traditional trade rules on access to markets holds up very nicely, because Article III of GATT—the so-called national treatment arrangements—prohibits putting on an internal measure, which has the exact same effect as the import control. If a country happens to put a domestic excise tax on all its coffee, which some countries have done and gotten away with, under the GATT rule that is prohibited just as much as putting an import duty on the same coffee by a same or equal amount. So one could easily imagine a rule difficult to negotiate, difficult to implement, but moving in the direction I would like to move, which would be precisely analogous.

That is what the Jamaicans have done in bauxite. They have not put on an export tax. They have put on a production levy. Now, all the bauxite happens to get exported either in raw or processed form. And so it is exactly equal to an export tax, which I would like to put some rules on. It is tough. But it has to be tackled for exactly the reason Martin said.

Henry Costanzo

Lincoln Gordon assumed in his paper, as did the panelists in their commentaries, that the amount of capital—equity, debt, and otherwise—moving into mineral production has diminished sharply. Is there a factual basis for this assumption?

Willis Armstrong

I don't have any numbers, but I know from talking with people in business that what happened in the boom of 1972-73 was essentially not sustained long enough to lead to a market judgment to warrant a great expansion of supply to meet such a sustained boom. The boom simply did not last that long.

Besides that factor, there is the factor of nationalization all around the circuit. Every major international mining company has encountered nationalization, some with compensation, some without, and some with compensation that was later revoked. Therefore, they are all pretty weary of it. If you ask mining people (the Mining Congress is one of the best places to get papers on the subject) about what they see in terms of a long-term trend of the demand for copper or any other basic minerals, they will say that obviously there has to be a correlation with the growth of population. And, therefore, although the demand may not be noticeable this year or the year after, in due course that demand is going to express itself, unless there is some major technological change that will obviate the need for a particular mineral or metal.

To some extent, there is competition, for example, between copper and aluminum. And, therefore, the bauxite price rise can render some benefit to copper producers. Fundamentally, the mining people talk about a lack of available capital, and a lack of interest. A lot of them will move into the kind of thing Fred Bergsten is talking about; and, obviously, that is what's going to happen if there is going to be mineral development in a lot of the developing countries. That is the only way it is going to happen. Some of this capital will be borrowed from the Eurodollar market and some of it may be equity from IFC or someplace. But I doubt that, in terms of equity, there is going to be much out of the private capital markets. I think that most mining companies have recognized long ago that the future of equity in developing countries is simply no good, as have the oil companies.

I might make a comment on oil. There is a snag in this capital development matter. Oil companies, as former concessionaires, have been reduced to a minority position with, say, 49 percent and the host country has 51 percent. The host country can decide that it wants to go ahead with a very substantial expansion program. It may be a country that has more cash than people and it decides to increase the capital investment by X percent and it turns to the company that it just expropriated and says, "You are a 49 percent owner and here you have put up 49 percent of the capital." This may be totally contrary to the judgment of the oil company in terms of the best place to put its capital. It might prefer to put its capital in Alaska or in the North Sea.

Lincoln Gordon

I did not say "diminished sharply," because I do not know the facts. But I have a strong impression that the rate of investment in minerals in developing countries has gone down. I also have the impression that, as one moves toward very substantially lower grade ores, capital requirements tend to increase. There are indications that capital investments required for minerals development are increasing more rapidly than overall price levels. Perhaps one of my colleagues has a factual answer to the factual question.

Willis Armstrong

I would like to try to comment on that, having been in the trade and commodity area back in the 1940s in the State Department.

There was a high suspicion among U.S. policy people in the economic field in the period 1945-47—a very high suspicion of commodity agreements, because commodity agreements to them meant the diamond cartel, the rubber cartel, the tin cartel, and all the other private and public or semipublic arrangements that had been worked out before World War II by Europeans over commodities that the United States imported. Therefore, there was a very strong prejudice against things called "commodity councils." This was also a viewpoint very strongly put forward by the business community. Everybody would cheerfully say one reason we did not have any rubber in World War II and the reason we were unable to fight the war effectively was the cartel scheme, operated by the British and the Dutch in the period before the war. This may not be a rational kind of explanation, but there was a very strong psychological factor of strong opposition to commodity agreements.

Therefore in the ITO charter (the charter was drafted by the United States) was the proposal that grudgingly said, "Well, if people are going to have commodity agreements, then let it be clear that there will be equal representation by consumers and producers, that there will be no effort to distort or subvert any basic market trends. And let these arrangements be made on an open basis."

Now, the further point, again, particularly a U.S. point, is that the United States cannot enter any commodity agreement without a specific judgment by Congress. This has been quite an inhibiting factor and therefore the executive branch has always tried to avoid any kind of general commitment to get too involved in commodity agreements.

A more specific recent example is the question of the Cocoa Agreement. The United States had a chance to sign the Cocoa Agreement about 1973. The judgment was that the Cocoa Agreement

would never get through Congress. Therefore, it was thought better
to suggest to the cocoa negotiators that they negotiate the kind of an
agreement that did not require U.S. participation, which is what had
been done for tin earlier. This is the way it was done. The price
of cocoa has been well above the prices of any agreement ever since,
so it has not been relevant. Now, a new agreement has been negotiated and the market is still above the agreement price. So, again,
it is still not relevant. But, although this second effort came after
the September 1 speech in the UN, I notice that the United States has
just said it will not go along with the current proposal for a Cocoa
Agreement. It just has to be recognized that in the United States,
certainly in the business circles, there is a very strong ideological
sentiment opposed to international commodity agreements. If the
U.S. government is going to sign or subscribe to any agreement,
it has to engage in a very major effort with the industry concerned,
and it has to have compelling reasons to accept an agreement.

   At the moment, the United States has said it will sign the agreement. But the steel industry, which is the primary consumer of tin,
is firmly opposed to the United States signing. How effectively it
will make its opposition, I do not know. The cost impact on the steel
industry is minimal, absolutely minimal, but its ideological objection
is strong.

David Pollock

   I would like to return just for a moment to a question that I had
posed earlier in my original presentation, but which was not then
answered because of the time limit. I would now like to rephrase
it.

   Our panel was supposed to concentrate on global commodity
policies and global international organizations designed to implement
such policies. I think Lincoln Gordon used the phrase "the international economic order" in this context as part of the title of his
paper. So, I would like to ask the following questions: Could someone give me their opinion as to why only two of the three institutions
recommended by Lord Keynes in 1942 eventually materialized?
Why did the third one, the General Commodity Council, never see
the light of day? Does anyone in this colloquium feel that now,
just a month before the Paris Conference on International Economic
Cooperation and only six months before UNCTAD IV, a General
Commodity Council is in fact worthy of international support? I
gave some reasons a moment ago as to why I thought it was. I am
curious to know whether anyone else feels the same way.

Walter Sedwitz

   I think Lincoln Gordon's paper is an outstanding contribution to
the understanding of this very complex problem. I find myself a
little bit uncomfortable, because all the other speakers have been
so convincing that I am not quite sure where I, personally, come
out.
   I do want to make one or two comments, though. First, to get
it out of the way, I want to comment on the institutional part. I fear
that, apart from the proverbial fatigue of creating new institutions,
we now have basically two types: those that are mainly political or
in which economics really becomes politics and those that are financial institutions in which politics obviously enters, but in which it
becomes a very small, perhaps marginal, element.
   I fear very much that the former type very often becomes group
therapy or wailing walls, in which there is a kind of an escapism
where complaints and difficulties are articulated, while the latter
has proven to be useful in terms of getting the United States and
other developed countries to focus on certain problems.
   These institutions, if they are to be agile, have to have a small
membership. And if they have a small membership, a lot of countries consider them nonrepresentative. This causes the dilemma
of how to make them both agile and representative, and I do not
think it is possible to reconcile the two aspects.
   Basically, my own preference would be that we retain the
institutions we have and try to modify them, in the way that Fred
Bergsten has spoken and written about reforming GATT. This is
preferable to moving into a jungle of new institutions, which would
all have to start from the beginning and which, in turn, would, of
course, also feel that they have to create new approaches and
duplicate and repeat what other institutions have done. In the field
of natural resource development, I see tremendous possibilities
precisely on the part of the international financial institutions, such
as the World Bank, the American Development Bank, IFC, and
others. It is quite true, and this is implied in the discussion, that
the rate of investment by the developing countries, and I stress the
rate of investment in natural resource development in the developing
countries, is declining. In Latin America, the decline is not very
important, mainly because of the efforts that have been made in
Brazil to come to grips with this problem. In other countries, such
as Chile, Peru, and Venezuela, the situation is different.
   I agree with Willis Armstrong that over the next 25 years at
least we are going to see tremendous capital shortages. They are
already manifested in interest rates, as everyone scrambles for

more capital. But I think worthwhile projects and enterprises will always be able to get some capital, and I think the combination of international financial institutions combining their financing with the private sector is perhaps the best prospect.

In this connection, I refer to some new methods of financing, for example, the Inter-American Development Bank cofinancing with a group of private banks that are purchasing participations in the project. More than that, the various initiatives put forward in the Development Assistance Committee and the Inter-American Development Bank attempt to deal with this problem on a concrete and practical basis. Guarantee funds have been proposed and now are under discussion.

For example, I could visualize through these guarantee funds access to capital markets with an arrangement whereby a private company in the United States will take up not an equity in a mining venture but a bonded issue from the country. This bonded issue would be guaranteed by international financial institutions, and the enterprise that takes up the bonded issue would in turn sell its technology and perhaps management to the local enterprise.

In other words, there are ways of dividing equity investment from the transfer of technology—which is absolutely necessary in the development of natural resources—where the investor minimizes his risk by direct ownership in the enterprise. It may be possible to minimize this risk by the guarantee provided by the international financial institution. In summary, in the development of natural resources, the financial institutions seem to me the most promising. I can envisage the possibility of a much larger volume of mineral development, or natural resource development as a whole, through some combination of international financial institutions, private capital markets, and enterprises in the developing countries, with government guarantees.

IV

**PROSPECTS FOR
INTERNATIONAL ORGANIZATIONS
IN THE AREA OF
INTERNATIONAL TRADE**

MANAGING INTERNATIONAL
TRADE
Harald B. Malmgren

ECONOMIC INTERDEPENDENCE

While it has become commonplace to speak about our "global
village" and about the intertwining of our respective national economies, until fairly recently the issues of international economics
and domestic political economy were handled quite separately in
the U.S. decision-making system. Indeed, it would be fair to say
that each separate question of economic consequence tended to be
handled separately, by different people, in different committees in
Washington. Internationally, different types of institutions were
developed in the mid-1940s and thereafter to deal with different types
of economic problems. The early separation of monetary matters
from trade matters, with the creation of two separate institutional
systems, was reflective of the differences in approach within the
national capitals.

As time went on, other types of institutions were created,
some with a regional purpose, as OEEC (Organization for European
Economic Cooperation) or the European Payments Union; and some
with global orientation but a specified set of objectives or mission,
as UNCTAD (UN Conference on Trade and Development) or the
Committee of Twenty in the pursuit of monetary reform under the
auspices of the International Monetary Fund (IMF) in the early 1970s.
In some of these bodies, such as in OECD in the 1960s and 1970s,
and in IMF, domestic economic policies were discussed to compare
notes on assessments of economic outlook and to provide an informal
occasion to compare experiences.

More recently, there have been many new bodies created, each
as a response to particular crises or challenges: some global, as
with the environmental conferences of the UN or the Law of the Sea

Conference; some regional or related to particular types of countries, as the International Energy Agency in Paris; and some bilateral, as the U.S.-USSR or U.S.-Saudi bilateral councils or commissions. As time goes on, this process increasingly resembles nuclear fission—a kind of chain reaction. Henry Kissinger's speech to the Seventh Special Session of the General Assembly on September 1, 1975 contained not only a multitude of economic proposals but also suggestions for a dozen or so new international institutions.

In the meantime, the interweaving of the U.S. economy with the world economy has accelerated without much attention to the consequences for institutional procedures or domestic decision making. As trade grew for more than two decades at roughly twice the rate of the gross national product for the major trading nations, national economies became increasingly enmeshed. As communications systems improved, ideas and capital moved faster and faster, with developments in the London and Paris markets affecting New York and Tokyo within minutes—even seconds.

Because the U.S. economy was so big relatively for so many of the years after the second World War, the international economy did not appear to affect the domestic economy. To the extent there was an interaction, it appeared to flow in the reverse direction, from the domestic decisions to international implications. Trade and investment, until recently, played only a very small role in the U.S. economy. In recent decades, import trade averaged below 3 percent of the gross national product. There was an exceptional rise during the Korean War period, but the average rose only slightly and only recently, during the 1964-70 period. By 1970, the ratio was still less than 4 percent. By 1974, imports stood at over 7 percent, and exports were at a similar level. Investment internationally was also not very significant until recent years. Even as recently as 1946, private long-term investment overseas was $12.3 billion, of which direct investment was $7.2 billion. In 1973, direct investment alone stood at $107.3 billion, nearly 15 times as large as the 1930-46 average level. Even so, the proportionate impact on the U.S. economy declined. It was not until the 1970s that the income derived from U.S. overseas investments began to exceed by substantial amounts the annual investment outflow.

As far as the dollar itself was concerned, the dependence of the world economy on U.S. aid, trade, and investment during and after World War II meant dependence on the dollar as the principal reserve currency. Since the dollar was a reserve currency, and the international monetary institutions were built around the dollar as the peg for other currencies, the United States could do what it wished for a long time, without concern for the effects of domestic actions on the dollar in world markets.

It was only dimly perceived in the late 1960s that monetary markets could no longer be insulated and managed separately around the world, and only in the beginning of the 1970s that international demand became a visible determinant of domestic price levels for raw materials and many manufactures and processed products.[1] The worldwide boom and the run-up of commodity prices, even before the sharp upward adjustment of oil prices, had a major impact on the internal U.S. economy. The linkage on August 15, 1971 of domestic price controls, investment incentives, gold to the dollar, and import surcharge was remarkable in the sense that it was recognized that the domestic and international aspects of the economic situation were linked at all.

In the 1970s, interdependence has also grown for other nations. In 1974, exports amounted to more than 20 percent of the gross national product in 8 of the 13 largest industrial countries. Ten years earlier, only 3 of these same 13 countries had ratios of exports to gross national product over 20 percent.

By the mid-1970s, following the oil price shock, and in the face of common recession on a scale deeper than any postwar recession, the major trading nations were beginning to contemplate economic summitry as a means of coordinating economic thinking, at least to some limited extent, and to demonstrate politically to national audiences that the respective economies had indeed become inter-dependent. There was great concern in the mid-1970s about which country would lead the recovery—hopefully, it would be the United States—and which countries would have to rely on export-led growth in response to the recovery of the markets in other nations. By the mid-1970s, the developed countries were concerned enough about the potential for restrictive actions, in the face of recession and inflation, to work out with each other a "standstill pledge" in OECD— a commitment not to take trade measures for balance-of-payments reasons or for general macroeconomic reasons. This ad hoc pledge was symptomatic of the new-found interest in mutual restraint in the handling of the economic crisis.

The turbulence of this period of the 1970s was nonetheless severe, and there were many specific trade-restrictive actions taken in the midst of market gyrations and structural adjustment throughout the world economy.

MANAGING INDUSTRIAL TRADE AMONG
THE DEVELOPED NATIONS

Although there were strong temptations to resort to unilateral actions to manage trade accounts among the various industrialized

nations during the 1970s, the pattern of liberalization set in previous
years held steady, except for narrowly defined actions in particular
sectors. There was enormous protectionist pressure, but the various
governments, in particular, the U.S. government, got the pressures
channeled and under control.

How this happened is a long story.[2] The end of the Kennedy
Round of trade negotiations came in the spring of 1967. By the
summer of that year, protectionist pressures were building rapidly
within the United States, and by the autumn, U.S. representatives
urged in Geneva the beginning of a new Work Program to identify
and analyze the remaining world trade problems. This was, in
effect, an attempt to go on the offense in order to defend against
protectionism at home. Domestically, a long process of consensus
formation in favor of new forms of liberalization was set in motion
by various farm and business groups and by the prodding of certain
members of the House and Senate. Internationally, the Work Program
provided a basis for common-sense discussions of how to hold steady.
The exchange rate crisis of 1971 led to pledges by the United States,
the European Community, and Japan to get moving multilaterally.
It then took two years, from 1972 to 1974 at the end of the year, to
get legislation enacted appropriate to a new international effort.
Intensive negotiations on a variety of bilateral trade problems during
this period demonstrated to Congress a seriousness of purpose and
it demonstrated that GATT (General Agreement on Tariffs and Trade)
rules and procedures, whether pursued bilaterally or multilaterally,
could be made to work. Even when the recession hit hard throughout
the Western market economies, the momentum built up over the
previous seven years was maintained. By late 1974 and 1975, the
developed nations were viewing the Multilateral Trade Negotiations
in Geneva as a process of control over national protectionist pressures, and some governments viewed this aspect of the negotiations
as more important than potential liberalization results that might
ensue in the late 1970s.

The negotiations in Geneva were intended to deal with the hard
issues that had been left behind in previous rounds of international
negotiations: the hard-core tariff questions, the nontariff measures,
the basic agricultural policy disputes, the rules of the game. The
GATT secretariat was called on to service these new negotiations,
but a deliberate step was taken to establish the negotiations as an
independent exercise among nations that decided they wanted to
negotiate. This formula left the door open for non-GATT countries,
and many of them participated.

After several years of careful preparatory work under the GATT
Work Program, and in the preparatory bodies precedent to the
formal initiation of negotiations, the complexity of the remaining

trade issues became better understood. This, in turn, led most
delegations to reassess how long it would take to negotiate new rules
of the game. In particular, the nontariff issues were found to involve
a close interweaving of domestic and international economic, regional,
and social policies. Actions taken for domestic reasons alone often
turn out to have an adverse effect on trade and therefore on the
interests of other nations. In such fields as regional aids to industry,
government procurement policy, and health and safety standards,
the international aspects were vital to world trade because of their
effect on the conditions of access to markets.

The complexity of these questions posed hard problems for
national governments: How to get decisions within their own political
systems to alter national measures; how to negotiate reasonable
bargains in connection with immeasurable issues; how to reorient
world trading rules realistically without impinging on the basic
requirements of independence and national sovereignty.[3]

The question of what to do about nonparticipants has not yet
been faced, but this, too, is a key question. If "free riders" are
allowed, many governments will fail to make the hard decisions,
and simply reap the benefits of negotiations among other nations
through the effects of the most favored nation (MFN) principle.
So the concept of cooperators as distinct from noncooperators had
to be developed for each area of trade agreements. (The Trade Act
of 1974 anticipated this problem by providing that nontariff barrier
agreements might be applicable to signers without necessarily being
applied to nonsigners.)

This issue in turn worried many governments, as they viewed
a change in the world trade forces in the mid-1970s. Increasingly,
the problems of oil and oil products seemed to be displacing the
traditional GATT questions. An International Energy Agency was
formed in Paris to cope with potential crises. A new "dialogue"
among the developed nations, the OPEC nations, and selected
developing nations was put together in Paris. Then there came an
intensification of the long-standing effort by developing nations to
resolve the problems arising out of their heavy dependence on
exports of primary products (discussed in the next section of this
chapter).

Some governments questioned whether liberalization could be
meaningful in trade if currencies were allowed to fluctuate widely,
neutralizing or offsetting the effects of tariff reductions and changes
in trade measures. The momentum built up over several years
served to keep the Geneva exercise going, but officials in capitals
continued to generate new institutional initiatives in other places to
solve specific problems as they came up or as they came to attention.

Thus this process of managing trade among the industrialized nations has been more stable than might have been expected. It is also subject to a momentum built up from forces that were set in motion several years before, when circumstances were different.

Internally, in each country the policies are subjected to pressures from myriad independent interests among farmers, workers, companies, banks, and government agencies, sometimes working directly and sometimes through members of Congress or Parliament in the country concerned. Trade measures affect specific institutions and people, as compared with broad foreign policy measures and positions, which affect moods and attitudes, but have little effect on the day-to-day economic circumstances of people or businesses.

This in turn tends to cause proliferation of committees, and large memberships on committees, for coordinating trade policy inside as well as outside government. This complexity combines with the slow and powerful force of the momentum built up in trade policy to create conditions preclusive of fast or timely policy decisions. Tensions have been growing between Congress and the executive branch in recent years, and in part the problems arise from the complexity of the issues and the special interests involved with them; in part from the sheer size of the system of public and private views and positions relative to the small number of people who can be expected to manage trade policy; and in part from the intertwining of domestic and international interests of the United States, bearing in mind that the international interests do not have many domestic votes.

MANAGING INDUSTRIAL TRADE AMONG
DEVELOPING NATIONS

Trade is an important element in the evolution of developing economies. There have been arguments in recent years that inward-looking development strategies make more sense for many developing nations, and that trade should not be considered a major determinant of domestic economic policy. For example, Mahbub ul Haq has argued that:

> policy-makers from the developing world generally throw up their hands in despair and frustration every time one mentions outward-looking strategies. They come out with a handful of statistics and a long litany of terrible experiences they have had in gaining access to the markets of the developed countries.

Basically, outward-looking strategy, while attractive
in principle, is still a very high-risk strategy. It assumes
that the developed countries are also likely to become
outward-looking. . . . On the other hand, import-substitution
strategy carries fewer risks for the harassed policy-makers
because high-cost goods produced under protective walls
can still be shoved down the throats of the local populations
by closing down any decent alternative.

The alternative strategy is what is described as inward-
looking, though such a description is often resented by many
of its advocates. This is generally the preferred operational strategy in many developing countries, even though
it is attacked with considerable vehemence by the academic
community.[4]

However, whether an outward-looking or an inward-looking trade
policy is adopted, recent experience clearly indicates that no nation
can insulate itself completely from world economic forces. Increasing
economic interdependence has helped pull along the growth of developing nations in times of boom in the industrialized nations, but it has
also brought severe declines in economic activity when world business
conditions were on the downturn. Interdependence has meant rising
prices for fuels, food, fertilizers, oil products, and capital equip-
ment imported from the rest of the world; and for those developing
nations highly dependent upon one or a few primary products for their
export earnings, the earnings from exports often have not kept pace
with the rising costs of basic imports.

The "tilt" of policy toward inward-looking or outward-looking
concepts should be judged in the context of the particular economic
and political circumstances of individual nations. Generalizations
on this subject have provoked an interesting but interminable academic
debate. It seems to me better to set aside this question, and instead
focus on the fact that increasing global economic interdependence has
a major effect on all developing nations, even those that follow
inward-looking strategies and that have highly protected, insulated
consumer goods markets. Clearly, some foreign earnings or foreign
development assistance is needed for economic development in every
case—the degree of external need varying from country to country.
Clearly, too, development assistance is still in trouble, with aid
flows from the richer nations well below hoped-for targets. Trade
is consequently important, and for good or ill, constitutes more
than four fifths of external sources of foreign exchange for the
developing world as a whole.

The experience of the 1970s so far has been that interdependence
and major structural readjustments in the world economic system

have combined to create economic turbulence of a kind not experienced since before the second World War. The exchange rate adjustments following the Smithsonian Agreement combined with strong demand and high rates of inflation in the developed nations to create an exceptionally strong demand for the raw materials exported by the developing nations. Most commodity markets strengthened—before oil prices moved up sharply. World grain markets, pulled by rising demand and by a concatenation of events ranging from disappearance of fish off the coast of Peru to drought in Canada and Australia, and boosted by the change in farm policy inside the United States and by the emergence of the Soviet Union as a major buyer, moved to price levels that were multiples of previous experience. Then the quad-rupling of oil prices came, long after these other forces were in motion.

The shock of all these adjustments brought about closer syn-chronization of the business cycles in the industrialized world, and the raw material markets, as had always been the case, moved up and down with the phases of the ensuing cycle. Primary products consti-tute the dominant portion of export earnings of the developing nations, so these market gyrations were quite important to their own internal economic developments. Exports of manufactures from the develop-ing nations only amounted to 13.2 percent of their total exports in the 1965-67 period. By 1971, manufactures had risen to about 23 percent of their exports. In 1974, manufactures had shrunk to 16.3 percent again, because of the shift in the relative position of oil.

Suppose for a moment we concentrate our attention on the non-oil-producing developing nations. From 1971 to the first half of 1974, these countries as a group were able to expand import volumes by 12 percent per year and still increase their reserves by more than $10 billion (in real terms).[5] The terms of trade of these countries grew with the general rise in raw materials prices, even though prices of manufactures were also rising rapidly. By 1974, the world market had shifted. However, due to the time lag between movements in prices and actual export earnings, the nonoil producers taken together still were able to increase their import volume and add to reserves in the first half of 1974. Then the picture completely altered. In the second half of 1974, the trade balances of these countries deteriorated sharply, even though import volumes also fell off. They were able to finance the deteriorating situation by drawing on reserves slightly and by borrowing abroad. In the first half of 1975, reserves declined by at least $650 million. The outlook is for continued deterioration, decline in reserves, and increased borrowing (for example, trade credit and commercial bank lending).

This problem of the non-oil-producing nations (or fourth-world poor countries) could have a most severe impact on many of the countries involved. It will also affect world trade as a whole, and perhaps world banking activities as well. Surprisingly, world trade declined in volume in late 1974 and early 1975 after decades of uninterrupted growth. Even more surprisingly, the only area of trade growth in late 1973 and early 1974 was due to the import demand of the developing nations.

There was a sharp break with postwar trends and patterns:

> The mutual trade of industrial countries, just over a half of world trade in 1973, was nearly stagnant in real terms while the volume of industrial countries' exports to developing areas, roughly one-eighth of world trade in 1973, expanded by an estimated one-quarter. The 5 percent increase in the volume of total exports of developing areas was achieved despite a decline in the volume of petroleum exports. Within this total, exports towards industrial areas, historically the more rapidly growing flow, increased markedly less than the rest in 1974, by not more than 3 percent. It follows that the mutual trade of developing countries grew at more than double this rate, the buoyant demand of the oil-exporting developing countries being the main element of dynamism in this flow.[6]

Another interesting aspect of this set of developments is that the financing of trade and commercial lending to governments, which has been a growing and profitable part of international banking activities in recent years, is vulnerable to the squeeze now taking place on the developing nations, and that the impact may be bigger than is widely recognized, since much of the recent growth in financing has been primarily with developing nations.

This background is essential to assessing the outlook for the developing nations in the longer term. Other papers for this conference have reviewed the food and raw material situation. I shall focus on the industrial products area.

To begin with, the dominant role of primary products in the exports of developing nations has to provide a point of departure. To the extent that a shift in the composition of exports is to be achieved, that shift will, in the aggregate, have to build on the resource base.

Various elements of the Kissinger proposals put forward to the Seventh Special Session of the General Assembly of the United Nations on September 1, 1975 could be helpful in relieving the financial predicament of the nations that import oil and rely for exports on primary products. It is conceivable that the case-by-case approach to commodity agreements will also bear fruit in some cases.

Realistically, however, diversification of exports and improvement of the quality of exports must be a central element of any new
economic program. Diversification of exports can include diversification of products and diversification of markets. Improving the
quality of exports means moving up the industrial ladder to provide
greater value added and more employment within the developing
nations as well as developing technologies and products that sell in
sophisticated markets.

A shift of this type involves structural adjustments throughout
the world economic system, changes in the trading rules, and
especially some adaptation of the trade policies of the industrialized
nations. At the present time, Multilateral Trade Negotiations
are underway in Geneva. The opportunity exists for negotiating
reductions in barriers to developing country exports in these negotiations.

First in priority in present discussions has been the conditions
of access for tropical products. Here the United States has been
forthcoming so far, and the other developed nations have made
appropriately sympathetic noises. The difficulties will arise when
nontariff impediments to trade, such as import quotas and domestic
excise taxes (very high and discriminatory in parts of the European
Community), are discussed; and when products that are also produced
in the United States, such as citrus products, come onto the agenda.

Of greater importance in the long run are other issues that, so
far, have been given little thought and less attention. First among
these is the structure of tariff protection in the industrialized
economies. Duties on raw materials are usually low in the major
trading nations, but tariffs on semiprocessed products are significant,
and tariffs on finished or fabricated products are much higher. The
objective of this tariff escalation is to provide incentives to perform
processing in the industrialized countries, so that the value added
generated is at home and not in the supplying country. The United
States is protective in this way, but so is the European Community.
Canada and Japan are even more protective of their processing
industries. While Japan may be able in the long-run to reduce its
protection and rely on more processing abroad, because of the
strength of its economy and its lack of land and labor and its pollution
problems, Canada, on the other hand, can be expected to want to
encourage far more processing within Canada of its own raw materials
The need for action to encourage a structural adjustment over time
to more processing in the countries of origin of raw materials is
great—it makes economic sense—but little has been done to facilitate
international discussion, and the resistance of industry to change in
some areas is likely to be great.

Even more important, however, are the tendencies in the industrialized nations to react against expansion of imports from developing countries by introducing new forms of protection or by raising levels of protection. There tends to be particularly great sensitivity because of the nature of the imports from developing nations. In manufactures, the exports most likely to penetrate developed country markets are those for which the labor content is high. These products consequently are likely to displace, or put pressure on, similar high-labor-content products produced in the importing country. Moreover, these workers are probably low-wage, low-skilled workers in labor-surplus regions in the developed countries—which is why the labor content is high. Sometimes the problem is aggravated by concentration of the exporters on the low quality, low-priced end of the product spectrum, forcing completely out of the market the low end of the product spectrum in the developed countries at a pace that greatly exceeds the general rate of increase of imports in relation to domestic consumption and production taken as a whole.

The tendency to introduce new protection or increased protection takes many forms. The traditional device of resorting to "escape clause" action and raising tariffs is not so likely to be employed, because tariff increases do not offset the price advantages sufficiently, and escape clause actions give rise to "compensation" negotiations. Instead, there is resort to requests for "voluntary" export restraint, or there is imposition of import quotas, or businesses in the field apply restrictive business practices to discourage marketing of low-priced imports (the latter technique used in Europe often).

To a limited extent, the developed countries have shown some willingness to discuss restrictions of this type in a multilateral context. The widespread quantitative restrictions on textile imports have led to discussions among the developed countries, and between them and the developing nations, culminating in a broad-based multifiber multilateral textile agreement under the framework of GATT. This agreement, on the one hand, approves restrictive action by the importing countries, but, on the other hand, provides guidelines for reasonableness in the imposition of the restrictions and for protection of the interests of the exporting nations.

In spite of this type of multilateral experiment, nations persist in going their own ways at the present time. The exercise of restrictive measures such as voluntary restraint agreements can be expected to grow in scope and importance. Therefore, it would seem imperative to negotiate in MTN some new ground rules for multilateral safeguard action that would guard against excessive protectionism, discrimination, and reversal of what has been accomplished by various forms of liberalization of tariff and nontariff barriers to trade.7 This would address more directly the "risk-aversion" problem posed by Mahbub ul Haq.

In the broader area of nontariff barriers and distortions to trade, there is much that could be accomplished to ease the difficulties of developing country exporters. It should be noted that nontariff measures probably cause less difficulty for the large, international trading companies and multinational enterprises than for smaller exporters, because the large exporters can and often do get around the difficulties by undertaking part of their activities in the market country, getting behind the nontariff barrier in question, or by using their superior legal and informational sources to find a way through the complex impediments.

In the nontariff area, the problems are extremely complex and intricately intertwined with domestic policy issues in each nation. I have discussed the questions in depth elsewhere and will not try to analyze the issues here.8 The relevance of the nontariff barrier area of discussion to developing nations, however, may be worth some examination. First among issues in contention at the present time, especially among the industrialized countries, is the question of export subsidies and the application of countervailing duties to these subsidies. Under GATT, countervailing duties may be applied to subsidized exports provided that injury is found. The U.S. law predates GATT and does not provide for an injury test. Consequently, most other nations concentrate their attention on the desirability of getting the United States to adopt an injury requirement.

The problems are not so simple, however. Export aids constitute a differential exchange rate for certain products. They constitute government assistance to private sellers, in competition with private sellers who do not have access to countervailing government assistance. Moreover, many export aids are intricately interwoven with domestic economic policies, such as regional aids for the promotion of industry in depressed areas and job-creation investment aids, which may result in promotion of export.

Moreover, given the special balance-of-payments problems and the artificial exchange rates and internal structural imbalances in their economies, the developing nations often resort heavily to use of tax incentives and other aids to exports to provide a favorable environment for export business. Most of the countries that have been most successful in developing exports of manufactures, among the developing nations, have resorted to extensive use of export incentives.

Recently, in the United States this practice has come into jeopardy, as domestic economic interests have brought actions against importers for the application of countervailing duties.

Brazil, Colombia, and Korea have been caught in this expanding net. On the other hand, the developing nations do have an interest (although they have not expressed this interest in meetings) in the development of a set of rules that would circumscribe the freedom of developed countries in the use of export aids. Obviously, the richer countries are in a much stronger position to distort markets with export aids than are the developing nations. Export aids on Italian tractors exported to North Africa in competition with tractors produced in some developing nations and exported to the same North African market will, in the long run, constitute a major problem for the developing country exporter.

The problem, therefore, is to encourage a code of conduct that defines legitimate practice and that circumscribes the developed country governments, and then to provide some kinds of special clauses that might allow, under special circumstances, the use of export aids by developing countries. This will not be easy. But without some action here, we can reasonably expect rapidly increasing application of countervailing duties, at least by the United States.

In the area of state-trading activities, little is being discussed in MTN. Yet this is a problem area, too. Many of the developing countries are increasingly reliant on use of state-owned or -managed producing and trading enterprises, and the pricing and marketing activities of these entities fall into a grey area between public and private rules of the game. For example, either antidumping or countervailing duty action could be applied to these cases, without any basis of knowing which would be used and when. Similarly, the broad question of government procurement policy, which is subject to intense discussion among the industrialized nations in OECD, but which has not yet emerged in MTN talks, brings up many questions of government policies that could have a large impact on developing country export opportunities and also on developing country internal government purchasing policies.

These kinds of questions are being given scant attention at the present time. They are complex. It would take two or more years to develop common concepts of the problems and commonly agreed solutions once a dialogue were engaged. So the delay and lack of attention can only mean a prolonged period of increased uncertainty and increased protectionism in the industrialized countries, further clouding the outlook for the developing nations.

The developing countries some years ago put major emphasis on the introduction of a General Scheme of Preferences by the developed countries. This idea was first suggested in the late 1950s by economic experts, and it was eventually agreed to on the U.S. side by President Lyndon Johnson at Punta del Este in 1967. It was not until the passage of the Trade Act of 1974 in January

1975 that U.S. implementation became possible and not until late 1975 that actual implementation could take place. In the meantime, the developing countries have lost some of their interest in this approach to assisting their exports, particularly of manufactures. This is just as well, because the preference schemes of the developed countries are unlikely to have a major effect on export performance; and if products do succeed too well, it safely may be assumed that the industrialized countries will exercise their escape clauses and return duties on such products to the MFN rates. In fact, the preference schemes will continue to be overshadowed by the possibility of such escape action and, even worse, by the possibility of voluntary restraint agreements that may be imposed on successful exporters.

Turning back then to some of the recent developments in trade trends that were discussed at the beginning of this chapter, I would like to highlight an issue that has been given very little attention in international academic or public policy debate. That is the question of promoting intradeveloping country trade. The trends noted earlier suggest that intradeveloping country trade may already be showing new promise.

Elsewhere I have recommended increased regional cooperation, particularly in the Asian-Pacific or Southeast Asian area, in part as a defensive measure against what I believed three years ago to be an increasingly hostile trading environment for the developing nations.[9] One can go beyond regional concepts, however, to the question of promoting intradeveloping country trade generally. Here I am thinking in particular of trade in manufactures and the related question of financing trade in this field. In some of the areas of manufactures, lead times and delivery times are the critical factors, but financing may often make the critical difference. Very little thought has been given to ways to encourage and assist financing of trade among these nations. It is a subject that could be gone into with benefit to all countries, particularly in connection with the heavy debt problem, and the growing problem of credit worthiness of these countries. Finally, and perhaps most important, are the protectionist policies of the developing nations themselves.

Finally, I should perhaps discuss the question of political and economic cooperation among the developing nations in their approach to bargaining with the developed nations. Until now the developing nations have pretty much stuck together and have allied themselves with the oil-producing nations. This makes political sense, but the economic differences are sharply divergent. They have relied on the rhetoric of justice and new world orders, on the domestic politics of blame and revenge, and on the political solidarity among them to substitute for concrete thinking about solutions to their own trading problems.

At this juncture, given the constructive approach of the Kissinger speech to the Seventh Special Session, and the opening of a broader dialogue in the Paris producer-consumer conference, the particular economic issues may finally come into focus after some several years of ideological and rhetorical debate. I consider the opportunities provided by this change in circumstance to be great. But I also think very little thought has been given to specific types of actions and solutions.

The old assumption that policies should simply be changed and adjustment assistance be provided for those adversely affected is far too simplistic, and in the present economic climate, adjustment assistance to cities or to people is equally unpopular and costly.

THE INSTITUTIONAL FRAMEWORK

By the early 1970s, we had an array of techniques for managing trade relations: bilateral problem solving through bilateral agreements or bilateral "commisions"; multilateral agreements, with rights and obligations, of which GATT is the principal example; multilateral policy harmonization through consultation, principally through OECD (as in preparation for meetings in GATT and UN bodies, consultations on economic policies, and ad hoc discussions on issues of current concern); and specialized multilateral bodies, of which UNCTAD was a major example and organizations like the Customs Cooperation Council, the Food and Agricultural Organization (FAO), the commodity organizations, and the regional organizations. Evolving over recent years at another level of interchange have been the self-contained regional trade groupings, of which the major example is the European Community and its special arrangements with associated nations.

Since then, many new bilateral, multilateral, and selective intergovernmental arrangements and institutions have been generated. Some of these were overlaid on the existing system, as in the case of the displacement of the old Group of Ten (the key industrial countries) with a new committee known as the Committee of 20 (the key industrial countries, plus key developing nations) within the IMF framework, whereas others were essentially new and different, such as the International Energy Agency (IEA) and the producer-consumer dialogue, otherwise called the Conference on International Economic Cooperation, launched in Paris in 1975.

We have already looked at the economic turbulence of the 1970s and the role of economic interdependence and overlap of national economies in the changing structure of the world economy. Are the systems for discussion and negotiation that we now have adequate to manage trade relations? Or should we create a new, overall economic institution on a global basis, with new rules and obligations?

This latter question is raised periodically by well-intentioned reformers who find the present confusion and multiplicity of institutions very untidy. The problem with bringing all of the issues in international economics under one new set of rules and one new organizational framework is that it would be almost impossible to negotiate. In other words, logic may suggest consolidation; but politically it may not be feasible without throwing away many of the old and valuable agreements in favor of new, vaguer understandings that could form the basis of consensus internationally.

When the IMF-World Bank-GATT systems evolved into their present form in the late 1940s and early 1950s, American hegemony and a small number of other activist countries combined to make negotiation of new procedures relatively easy. Today, more and more governments want to be involved in what is going on, and in particular in shaping new institutions or new world orders. The rapidly expanding multipolarity of the trading world is one problem. Side by side with it is the growing complexity of the economic issues: At home, in each economy, more and more affected parties are expressing views of their own; and internationally, among governments, expanding activism makes formation of international consensus more and more difficult.

In a sense, a stable system is one based on consensus that the system works. A stable system can be subject to gradual evolution and reform; but the key question is whether or not it works reasonably well in keeping a substantial degree of order in relations among nations. Formation of consensus is easier when the number of concerned parties is small, and where the objectives are similar. Where, as now, the number of players is great and their views on what is just vary widely, consensus formation will take a very long time.

As pointed out in the section on trade among industrialized countries, the evolution of the Trade Act of 1974 and the movement of the world from 1967 rising protectionism to 1975 trade negotiations took eight years. Within the trade area alone, a change in policy requires a buildup of momentum in the domestic political system and in the international institutions and in government-to-government relations.

The increasing interlinkage of domestic and international economic issues compounds the difficulties. Domestic price controls or incomes policies will tend to run into conflict with international demand pressures without intervention at the border. Government actions to shore up weak industries or take them over will create conditions of conflict with similar industries in other nations. As

we have seen above, synchronization of business cycles and the
rapidity of transmission of economic effects from one nation to
another have created conditions of turbulence in the world economy.

The increasing activism of governments themselves changes
the nature of the ball game. As governments increasingly intervene
to own, manage, control, or regulate their own resource exploitation
and their own economic development generally, the potential for
conflicts in national policies grows.

The size of daily problems also seems to be growing. The
impact of the entry of a state-trading nation such as the USSR into
grain markets ten years ago was not so great as to cause general
market disruption, whereas in the 1970s the same action has an
effect on a much larger and more pervasive scale. In the 1960s,
the organization of raw material suppliers to coordinate policies
posed no threat because their combined power was inconsequential
relative to the countervailing powers in existence at that time.
Today, coordination of policies can have major market effects,
whether the resulting actions are part of a conscious, coordinated
plan, or the result of tacit cooperation.

The proliferation of interlinkages between national decisions,
at home and abroad, has created a situation where the frequency of
policy decisions or policy problems is increasing.

So we have, as a consequence of the forces at work, expanding
multipolarity, increasing complexity of issues, interlinking of the
outcomes of decisions through the effects of increasing interdependence, intensified activism by governments, growing need for consensus
and growing difficulty in creating it, and increasing rate of policy
developments or developments that call for policy decisions. This
rapidly growing array of difficulties in the management of the system
is beginning to threaten the stability of the system. In the raw
materials area, for example, the public policy outlook throughout
the world is so uncertain that investment in needed capacity expansion
is not taking place, which simply intensifies the problems by creating
greater potential scarcities.

I would also like to note here the problems of time dimensions.
The time required to perceive a problem is often long. Data over
a period of time have to be collected before a new pattern becomes
visible. The time required to analyze newly emerging problems
and lay out options, taking into account the complexities noted above,
is more than minutes; it may even be years, as in the case of
examination of raw material outlook for an economy as large as
the United States or examination of energy needs and policy options.
Making a decision takes time, particularly if it must move up in the
system to high levels and be "scheduled," or if it requires implementing authorities from Congress. Making a decision may also require

development of a national consensus about what should be done, which may involve consultation with advisory bodies or may even involve extensive educational processes. Finally, the implementation of decisions may be a very lengthy process. Application of an import surcharge can be done almost at once; negotiation of a change in the international conditions can take years; and reorganization of domestic or international institutions always takes at least months, and usually years.

We are thus faced with the problem that public policy, reliant on momentum of ideas and positions of the many interested players, often overshoots or undershoots the target as the world economic circumstances change. The Trade Act of 1974, several years in the making, would have been drafted differently in 1975, in connection with the problems of 1975. GATT would be different today if it were drafted last year. The decisions of governments are often related to problems of another day, while problems of today are only dimly perceived. Rarely are the problems of tomorrow anticipated and dealt with—the best example being the awareness in Washington of the likelihood of rapid increases in oil prices in the mid-1970s many months before the October 1973, Arab-Israeli war and the subsequent oil embargo. (In the case of oil, the only surprise about the price increases was their rapidity and intensity, in a shorter time span than had been envisaged by the major oil companies and various government officials.)

The sovereignty of governments is also threatened by these various forces, because the forces seem to be beyond the control of individual government systems. As a consequence, some people argue that liberalization and economic "openness" have gone too far, and that the time has come for retrenchment, for insulation from uncontrollable external forces, for differentiation of policies. This line of thinking is embodied in concepts like the Burke-Hartke bill and in Gaullist policy reasoning.

I think that is a futile approach. Instead, I believe we must look at this area as we would the organization of our highly complex social and political systems, by trying to deal directly with what rules, customs, laws, and procedures are necessary to keep order. As I have said elsewhere

In trying to find a better system for managing economic interdependence while ensuring a large degree of freedom for national governments to deal with their own social and economic problems, one cannot help recalling the centuries-old philosophical debate about how to ensure freedom to the individual citizen in the context of orderly communal relations. The same kind of issues

arise in the management of international economic affairs
and one is drawn to the conclusion that real freedom for
a national government can only be found, in this highly
interdependent world, within a framework of international
rules, procedures and tacit or explicit understandings.[10]

While I recognize that the various international institutions all
serve different purposes, I now believe that a first step in getting
hold of the evolving forces would be to stop creating new institutions
and to put more emphasis on utilizing the existing ones better. This
does not preclude modernizing the present systems, nor does it
preclude consolidation of some of the discussions taking place in
many parts of the world.

In trade, I believe the separation of commodity issues from the
main outlines of industrial trade, by carrying on commodity discussions in forums other than GATT or MTN, is a mistake in the long
run. The interrelated character of services, trade in raw materials
and industrial trade, and government economic policies that affect
trade should be self-evident. It may also become evident that trade
and international business activity cannot readily be looked at
separately if governments really want to shape trade patterns or
control unexpected trade developments at least to prevent market
turbulence. The activities of multinational corporations and the
policies of governments that affect them and that affect the international placement of capital are now being looked at in OECD and
in the UN system. To me, there is an inescapable relationship of
these issues to trade issues.

Consolidation does not have to take the form of moving all negotiations and discussions to one forum. It can take place through
direct consultations among governments, although this becomes
very difficult the more the number of governments involved. It can
also take place through a conscious effort to provide an overview or
surveillance system.

In the same way that I expressed doubts about the wisdom of
trying to negotiate entirely new bodies, I would doubt the wisdom
of too rapid an effort to consolidate the issues formally. On the
contrary, there remain strong reasons for disaggregation of many
of the economic issues and negotiation of them in separate places,
wherever political rhetoric and political maneuver are dominating
the substantive issues. This is clearly the case for raw material
and commodity policy, with the industrialized countries and the
developing countries at loggerheads over philosophic questions,
without adequate attention to what the specific economic problems
of each nation are. At present, we see political alliances that bear
no relationship to the disparate economic interests of the countries
concerned.

However, there is need for some kind of overview where differentiation or disaggregation of issues takes place to ensure consistency, to ensure balanced progress on related issues, and to ensure that the political element is given scope to vent itself in constructive ways. Thus, I would favor an effort by the Special Session of the General Assembly to turn away from drafting of new world order documents and toward surveillance of the progress made in the various institutions working on the different economic issues. Alternatively, an ad hoc group such as the Paris producer-consumer dialogue could perform this function.

GATT might not like this, because the GATT system is not presently part of the UN family. It prides itself on its independence. However, I do not think that surveillance of what is being accomplished need impair its effectiveness. On the contrary, I would expect participation to grow as other nations gradually discovered the role and daily functions of the GATT system.

Pragmatism in shaping a new order may be necessary in other ways. The kinds of problems raised by negotiation on nontariff distortions to trade in terms of interlinked domestic and international policies cannot be permanently resolved by trading this restriction for that. New rules cannot be designed to take into account every eventuality, particularly at a time when public pressures for governmental action in the economy or in safety, health, consumer, and environmental standards are so strong. We need therefore to look for a system of rules that provides broad guidelines of reasonable behavior in each problem area, but that relies on a new type of ongoing consultative procedure to deal with the problems as they emerge concretely over time. What I mean by this is that the codes of conduct we write have to be combined with new consultative committees that serve a function somewhat like our courts—interpreting what the rules mean in specific cases. The body of deliberations, opinions, and judgments made in each case then become, through precedents, an elaboration of the general rules. In this way the system becomes a living entity, adapting as it goes along to changing circumstances.

This is even more true in looking at the particular problems of the developing nations outlined. Rewriting the entire set of trading rules to take care of developing country needs would, because of the politics and the uncertainties economically, result in a negotiating conference that would be at an impasse for many years, while in the meantime the existing rules, which provide a modicum of order, would lose their meaning.

If we also add the dimensions I have discussed of fundamental structural alterations in economic flows among countries and the concurrent problems of synchronized business cycles and general inflation, the possibility for designing a just system that would have lasting value seems remote. Unless, that is, the system is in some sense a self-adapting system that gradually increases the day-to-day consultative process among governments. No where has this been more apparent than in agriculture, where the problems are insoluble without some degree of policy harmonization or cooperation. Management of grain supplies in the absence of world reserves and with minimal U.S. stocks will test governments in coming years as it has in the last two or three years. But agriculture is only an example.

What I argue for, in other words, is an evolutionary rather than revolutionary approach. It is untidy, but it is practical. However, to make it work at all, there has to be substantial improvement in the domestic decision-making system in the United States itself, including substantial improvement in the congressional-executive relationship and the executive-private sector relationship. The present situation of confusion, lack of coordination, and bureaucratic competition is a situation of disarray inadequate for the needs of coming decades.[11] We could afford some slippage and some errors in the past. In the new world of growing interdependence, the disorganization in Washington will prove increasingly costly.

To the extent that such confusion also prevails in other capitals, the problems will be compounded. Without an overall concept of what the management should be, and how it should function in relation to specific issues, it is difficult to visualize anything but economic turbulence and ad hoc reactions, which may often prove to be over-reactions, or reactions to the wrong problems, or to the right problems at the wrong time. This prospect is made all the more threatening by the growing activism of governments in seeking achievement of more and more economic and social objectives, while striving to maintain sovereignty and rights of unilateral action. The present system is like an experiment designed to test the effects of pressure on a rigid container. We shall know how much pressure the system can take when we see the container crack.

NOTES

1. For a history of the period after the Second World War concerning the interaction of domestic and international economic policy of the United States, see my forthcoming chapter in W. Kohl, ed., National Economies and Economic Policies.

2. I have provided some of the background of the domestic and international maneuvers in a forthcoming article, "Sources of Instability in the World Trading System," Journal of International Affairs, Spring 1976.

3. For a full discussion, see M. J. Marks and H. B. Malmgren, "Negotiating Nontariff Distortions to Trade," Law and Policy in International Business 7, no. 2 (1975).

4. Mahbub ul Haq, "Industrialisation and Trade Policies in the 1970s: Developing Country Alternatives," in P. Streeten, ed., Trade Strategies for Development (London: Macmillan, 1973), pp. 93-96.

5. See OECD Economic Outlook, no. 17 (July 1975), pp. 60ff.

6. GATT, International Trade 1974/75, October 1975, p. 5.

7. I have discussed this need at length in International Economic Peacekeeping in Phase II (New York: Quadrangle, 1972); and in "The Impact of the Developed Countries," in P. Streeten, ed., Trade Strategies for Development (London: Macmillan, 1973).

8. See M. J. Marks and H. B. Malmgren, op. cit.

9. See, in particular, "Regional Cooperation: Why Is It Necessary?" Solidarity (Manila), October 1973; and "Trade Liberalization and the Economic Development of the Pacific Basin: The Need for Cooperation," in H. E. English and K. A. Hay, Obstacles to Trade in the Pacific Area (Ottawa, 1972).

10. "Need for a New System for World Trade and Payments," Ch. 6, in H. Corbet and R. Jackson, In Search of a New World Economic Order (London, 1974).

11. My views on the present situation are contained in my statement before the U.S. Senate Subcommittee on International Finance, Committee on Banking, Housing, and Urban Affairs published in "International Economic Policy Act of 1975," Hearings before the Subcommittee on International Finance, on S. 1262, to authorize appropriations for carrying out the provisions of the International Economic Policy Act of 1972, as amended; and in my statement on "Congress and Foreign Economic Policy," before the Special Subcommittee on Investigations, Committee on International Relations, U.S. House of Representatives, July 28, 1976.

8

INTRODUCTION
Harald B. Malmgren

I do not intend to go over all of my paper but will describe in brief what I tried to say. Part one is on economic interdependence. Part two is on managing industrial trade among the developed countries. Part three deals with the developing countries, and four discusses the institutional framework, which is what this colloquium is about.

At the outset, I have outlined the way in which institutions have evolved to deal with interdependence. As I pointed out, since the Second World War, many different kinds of institutions have been created, each with its own purpose. There was a certain tendency to separate issues; the separation of money and trade is a good example, but not the only one. There were also other kinds of separation, such as the regional institutions, OEEC or the European Payments Union, and institutions with a global orientation but more limited objectives, such as the Committee of 20 in the monetary field.

More recently, there has been a certain proliferation of new institutions: some global, such as the environmental conference of the UN or the Law of the Sea Conference; some regional, such as the IEA in Paris; some bilateral as the U.S. or USSR Saudi Bilateral Commission. As time goes on, it seems that this process resembles a chain reaction that is a bit out of control. The Kissinger speech to the Seventh Special Session had many suggestions for new institutions, probably at least a dozen new ones, on top of all the institutions that we already have.

In the meantime, it has been my observation that the interweaving of U.S. internal economy and the international economy has been taking place quietly and without much notice. I do not think, although there is an argument among the academics about this, that the domestic economy and the international economy were much intertwined in policy deliberations until about 1969. In 1969, the slowly emerging effects of the accumulation of dollars in Europe brought out major problems in monetary management, as dollar movements and the infringement of the Eurodollar market infringed on the freedom of the Federal Reserve in that year. Remember that the United States had a peculiar recession at that time that was out of step with the world economy, and a rise in interest rates was set in motion, against declining rates in Europe. The "shuttling" of Eurodollars which ensued was highly destabilizing on both sides of the Atlantic.

It was also not until about 1971 that major domestic and international issues were put together in a common economic program. Looking at the August 15, 1971 Connally measures, one finds both international and domestic measures in the same program on the same day presented as if they were all integral in fact. There is a certain logical relationship among the exchange rate, the investment incentives, and the price controls domestically—all being interconnected at that time. That was very unusual. If one goes back over the years, there are plenty of speeches referring to interconnection between domestic and international issues but very few examples of actual measures taken at the same time in an interwoven manner.

This interweaving really did not affect the United States too much in earlier years because the U.S. economy was relatively independent. Trade was a relatively small part of the gross national product. Investment was a relatively small factor until fairly recently. Overseas investment income was not big enough to stimulate policy or political interest until really the last couple of years. So it was possible for the United States to be separatist in its thinking, and it was possible indeed to make a lot of mistakes and not worry too much about the consequences because it did not really matter too much to the domestic economy. A certain amount of slippage could be afforded.

In that context, an acceleration of the interweaving of the economy is seen in the last two or three years. For a long time trade was growing at roughly twice the rate of the gross national product, which meant that the economies were becoming increasingly enmeshed. It has been during the last 20 years that this phenomenon has been seen. Then, in the early 1970s, it accelerated, which was surprising to everybody. Today there are about eight or ten major economies where the trade is more than one fifth of the gross national product, whereas there were only three economies at that level some years ago—Belgium, the Netherlands, and I have forgotten what the other one was at that time. The United States has almost doubled its proportion of trade to gross national product in two years, from 1973 to 1975. This coincided with the effects of world demand on the domestic economy, the price increase in commodities, the problems between price controls and export controls—general confusion.

With this background among the industrialized countries, I have tried to say something about how long it took to organize a policy that was based on domestic consensus and that was outward-looking between the end of the Kennedy Round until the Trade Act of 1974, which was really signed in January 1975. Basically, it took about eight years to achieve a position where protectionism, which was very definitely the strongest element in the domestic consensus, could be transformed into a somewhat outward-looking policy embodied in the act. This is a certain process, much like inertia in physics. It is hard to get something going, but once you do, it is hard to stop. Indeed you may go right past the problem you were trying to deal with because of momentum.

Concerning the Geneva negotiations, for example, many countries now say that the issues are interesting and it is a good thing that negotiations are going on, but they are not terribly relevant to the problems of today. Isn't energy more important, or isn't the monetary crisis for developing countries more important, and so forth. Increasingly we find ourselves dealing primarily with issues that intertwine domestic and international policy. Most of the nontariff issues relate to what governments want to do with their domestic economy by way of manipulation and in turn how that affects trade. So very basic questions of internal policy are raised. If we consider the issue of standards, there are health, safety, and consumer standards—the problem is to reconcile, internationally, what each government does. But, because you are dealing with domestic issues, the real issue becomes one of how to cope with the sovereignty question.

In regard to the developing countries, the problems are even more complicated. In the last couple of years, when the trade of the developed country economies went down for the first time since the war, the developing countries, in real terms, were still on the rise. In fact, the growth in world trade, in the 1974-75 period, was developing country trade and not all of the growth countries were oil-producing developing countries. In fact, the significant growth occurred in the developing countries' mutual trade. This was a peculiar development, a complete change in statistical patterns, and one can find a perceptible change in the position of the developed countries in world trade, as a percentage.

I then mentioned some of the problems that the developing countries have. Basically we find a set of problems that can only be dealt with by structural change, for example, changing the forms of protection, the tariff structures. In the areas where it would seem that progress is being made, the likelihood exists that this progress will be overshadowed by tendencies to use escape clauses or voluntary restraint agreements. We simply cannot presume that success in specific aspects of trade relations is going to last for more than a couple of years. Something will often happen to work against it.

In general, the areas in which the developing countries can move in diversification will tend to be the very areas that will create policy reactions in the developed countries. The use of a number of techniques for protection is being applied to developing countries for the first time in the last few years. For example, countervailing duties and dumping actions are now being utilized, although such instruments were not applied to these countries ten years ago. There is in fact now a proliferation of such cases. Escape clauses are also coming on stream. Negotiation is likely in the shoe area, and there will probably eventuate some form of restriction of shoe imports.

This area of commercial interaction with developing nations is also characterized by slow movement. I pointed out in passing that, like the Trade Act evolution, the generalized preferences started in the 1950s when the idea was considered among academics, and stretched into the 1960s when people like Sidney Weintraub were involved in the Executive Branch in intergovernmental discussions. Also in the mid-1960s, the "Wise Men's Group" conferred in Paris under the chairmanship of Mr. Sydney Goll of the United Kingdom. It was not until 1967 when President Lyndon Johnson finally committed himself and the United States to these preferences. At the end of 1974, it was finally possible to legislative authority, but even then it was not until the end of 1975 that implementation could take place. This again demonstrates how slowly new ideas move. Once momentum is established, there is movement, but it is not an easy process.

With that as background, I tried to get to the object of this meeting, which is what is the appropriate institutional framework. As I have said, there are a variety of international institutions, each geared to certain problems. A set of new and old forces is working against them, complicating the present situation quite a bit. The growing complexity of the economic issues, coupled with increasing interest in political circles and among interest groups who want to get involved with the decision making, creates conditions in which it is not easy to come to a decision any more. We find, moreover, trade associations, farmer groups, and other special interests in every country actively involved in the decision processes, much more today than 20 years ago. This does not mean that they are more effective, but it does mean that they are more active.

A substantial degree of order must be established in the international system, in spite of the exceptions and the manipulations of the rules and procedures by the various governments. The stability of the international system has to be supported by some kind of consensus between the governments and the people. Formation of consensus is much easier when the number of concerned parties is small and when the objectives are similar, as was the case at the end of the Second World War, when a small number of countries negotiated the institutions and were bargaining with a common objective. But consensus among a large number of players is much more difficult since the views in some cases are diametrically opposed to what is to be accomplished. Indeed, the views are quite a bit concerned with distribution of the gains of the system.

There is also an increase in linkage of domestic and international economic issues in many different ways: monetary, trade, food, the synchronization of business cycles, and the repeating of transmission of economic effects from one nation to another. An interest rate adjustment in London has an effect in Tokyo within seconds because of the computers and telecommunications systems used to make financial transactions worldwide. Even more important, the governments throughout the world are becoming increasingly active (particularly in developing countries) because people demand public action.

The size of the problems in each particular area is growing in relative importance. If the USSR had come into the grain market ten years ago, it would not have been a very disturbing thing. Today, for a variety of reasons, including the fact that we do not have adequate stocks in proportion to the scale of purchases, you have continuous potential for disruption in the market from rising food prices and wage-push problems that are consequent to escalating food prices. The scale of that kind of a problem hits us all in a way that it never did before.

Along with these kinds of developments, a growing array of difficulties arises in the management of the system and some underlying problems that increase the difficulties. For example, in the raw materials area, the public policy outlook is so uncertain that investors, whether public or private, governments or companies, are very dubious about increasing capacity; they do not know what governments will be doing or what the market will look like because it is government dominated. This makes the problem worse,

because to the extent that you do not increase capacity you ensure
that you will have scarcity over the longer term.

In addition to this, I want to note another problem—what I call
the time dimension. The time required in a government's process
of decision to perceive a problem is quite often very long. The
time to analyze a newly emerging problem and lay out the options
sometimes takes weeks, months, years. Data usually have to be
collected, particularly in the economic area, and people do not
believe something is a problem until they see a series, which takes
months or even years to generate. For example, in the raw materials
area, it has been taking years and is still continuing. Raising an
issue to some policy level where it has to be scheduled in competition
with a lot of other issues and then making that decision, which
requires some kind of consensus, national or congressional, takes
time. People have to be called and educated, meetings have to be
arranged, and documents have to be signed. Finally, an implementation of decisions takes time. You can, of course, apply an import
surcharge tomorrow morning or in 30-day notice, depending on how
you interpret the various acts. But negotiating a change in the system,
either in the international institutions or bilaterally with a government,
means preparing meetings, following up the meetings, and exchanging
documents. Reorganizing the institutions themselves is a very lengthy
process.

The question also arises: What is legitimate sovereignty for a
country? Many people argue that we have gone too far in opening
our economy. They feel all of this is evidence that we have done
too much by opening our economies through excessive liberalization,
that we have become too liberal, and that the time has come for a
retrenchment. It is sometimes argued that we need to build a dike
around each national economy, such as the United States, with
"sluice gates," which let some of the pressures through and keep
others out. You see this in many kinds of policies and philosophies.
It is consistent with some of the commission planning in the European
Community. I think it is futile to attempt to argue about it right now.
The interdependence has gotten so big, it is something you simply
cannot deal with through unilateral action.

The rationalist, somewhat moralistic, direction of trying to
find a rule of law or sense of stability in the system is a means of
keeping order in the social system. But I think that all of that
implies a certain moralistic notion that freedom is possible only
if you have a certain constriction on freedom. That is an old debate,
and since John Stuart Mill is not sitting here with us, I will not
get into it.

I think the problem with the one new body idea is that it is non-
negotiable. Because the numbers of countries involved are so large

and the objectives are so different, you could have an interesting
negotiating conference that would last many decades, but I do not
think you would have an institution. The process might lead to some
problem solving as you went along, but nothing substantial would
come from it. Therefore, let me say, I am an incrementalist. I
believe that you take what you have and you work with it. Anything
alternative is dreaming and impractical.

It is something like changing the law in the United States. You
do not try to rewrite the law, you add to it, subtract from it, shift
it around a bit. Sometimes you can reverse it completely by small
changes. But you work with the base you have.

I think that the issues in the trade field require some consolidation. I do not believe that separation of industrial trade from
developing country trade, and commodity trade from industrial
trade, and energy from commodity issues, makes any sense. In the
long run, I think those issues should be merged. The argument
presented by some of the countries in the Paris consumer dialogue
(that some of these things should be interrelated) is quite correct.
The U.S. position that it should be kept separate was either naive
or ignorant. The consolidation does not mean, however, that you
have put all things in one place, in a formal institutional sense.
What I mean by consolidation is that we have to think about the issues
and the relationship and talk about them in connection with one
another. I think that can be done either formally or informally.

Second, I think that you need a kind of political overview of
what is going on. Most of the rhetoric is generated by the developing
countries in particular and is related to political problems they have;
they are blaming somebody outside their own system for their predicament. Political need will be there as long as the domestic problems
exist, and you have to have a place to vent that steam. You cannot
shut it off. So there should be some kind of place where you can
talk about the general problems. That should be done in parallel
with the specific problems.

I think that you can apply that steam to good purpose by shifting
it away from drafting of a new economic order and charters to an
overview function. What is happening in each of the respective
institutions, and how do these things relate to one another? Is
there enough progress being made in X while Y is taking place?
That kind of political overview context could be done in a subcommittee, a special monitoring group of the general assembly.
This does not need to interfere with specific negotiation in separate
places. It allows consolidation of ideas and creates a certain degree
of order. It provides some place to vent that political steam that
is otherwise going to muddle the specific negotiations. GATT would
not like this in particular because it is not a part of the U.S. family.

So, the GATT secretariat will be very testy about being subject to reporting to any body at all. But I think that this is bureaucratic peevishness that is not too important a policy.

To put this together, then, let me say that the issues raised by negotiation of nontariff distortions to trade in terms of this inter-linkage of domestic and international cannot be permanently resolved—not by trading this issue for that issue nor this impediment for that—nor can you anticipate all of the kinds of problems that will evolve out of domestic economic policies over 20, 30, or 40 years. We will need to develop, in all of these areas, general rules about how you ought to behave so that the effects of your actions will not be felt adversely by another. We will have to set up procedures for particular cases. Those procedures will probably go on forever. And, if they stop somewhere, you are probably having trouble. They should be ongoing, similar in nature to how courts are to the law—precedence can build on one another and you gradually have a body of interpretation.

We also have to take into special account the case of the developing countries, because structural adjustments are very difficult to devise in advance and the future implications of these adjustments cannot be totally anticipated. There are obvious examples, such as agriculture, but in that area I think that it is simply impossible to make sense out of agriculture and manage grain supplies in any reasonable fashion without a much more intense intergovernmental discussion of policy and of management of supplies over the next two decades. And, of course, this interrelates with the question of reserves.

What I am arguing for is an evolutionary, rather than a revolutionary, approach—a great deal of pragmatism, a conscious notion of changing the institutions as you go along, a master strategy, and some kind of overview where you do articulate a direction. But we cannot try to create new institutions or replace the existing ones with the idea that everybody will cooperate, because it will not work.

I agree with a remark that Ray Cline made earlier. It would require a much more effective internal system of decision making in the United States than we have now. I do believe, based on my own limited experience in Washington, that this is the most confused period in the entire postwar period. The attempt even to coordinate issues is missing.

Now my colleagues will comment. On my right is Lawrence Fox, who was the deputy assistant secretary of commerce for international trade policy, under many, dozens anyway, of secretarys of commerce. He is one of the great figures of survival in the Washington system and one of the most knowledgeable people about trade policy that I know.

Maynard Glitman has been deputy assistant secretary for trade policy for some time. He was a close colleague of mine in implementing the present trade negotiations. He has a background in defense, as I do, and comes out of the NATO framework. So he has some quite interesting views, I am sure, on the institutional side of what should be done.

In introducing Walter Sedwitz, I just want to comment that Walter has been, over the years, one of the most effective people in trying to bridge the deliberations of the United States internally and the interest of the developing countries. His interest has mainly been with Latin America. He and I worked quite closely when I was in the executive branch, trying to develop what I call a dialogue with the Latin American countries on some of the issues—trying to find the areas of mutual interest and conflict and to develop some common concept of what ought to be done. Unfortunately, some of us had the idea that once the dialogue got going, and it seemed to be going somewhere, of having the secretary of state announce that we ought to have a new dialogue. We thought that might help the dialogue. Well, in fact, he announced the need for new dialogue in Mexico when this one was well underway. He gave it his blessing and the dialogue died for some reason.

COMMENT
Lawrence A. Fox

Many of the comments Harald Malmgren made were provocative, and I am tempted to leave my prepared thoughts to comment or rebut one or two of them. But I think I'll leave that for the discussion and stick to the way I've organized this subject in my own mind. I have viewed it somewhat more narrowly than his approach, and have tried to emphasize trade in industrial products, more particularly to compliment the earlier discussion on agriculture.

First, with respect to the observation that the world is now too interdependent and that we are suffering from the consequences, I am forced to observe or question, too interdependent for what? Certainly not too interdependent for the increases in real income that this sort of interdependence has created. And certainly not too interdependent in relationship to the economies of scale that are required for adequate utilization of new technologies and for the correct application of the amounts of capital required for the huge ventures that are necessary to produce the goods that we need to maintain a world population that is moving along at the rate that the population growth has been for the last several years and is likely to be for at least quite awhile in the future.

Therefore, I conclude that the problem is not to do away with interdependence in economic matters, and in particular in trade matters, but to seek better means of regulating the consequences of interdependence or managing the interdependence. My own way of saying this is that the degree of interdependence simply has outpaced the development of institutional arrangements with the necessary agreement on fundamentals to constitute the required basis for cooperation among countries.

I'm not going to say very much more about the organizational aspects of this problem, reserving that for perhaps later on. I would say right off, so that you know my prejudices and starting point, I don't believe in a supertrade organization. I don't believe that the problems of tariffs or nontariff barriers would be more readily solved if GATT and UNCTAD were combined or if there were a tin council meeting down the hall. I think a better degree of coordination could be achieved, but I'm not sure how essential even that is. I think what is really necessary—and that's the cliche I'm going to give you now—what is really necessary to move this thing along is some leadership in this world. I don't see where it can come other than from the United States. That was the situation in 1945, it was the situation throughout the postwar period, and it is the situation today in spades.

I agree with Malmgren that things have never been more confused—not only in this town, but around the world—in the focusing on specific objectives that countries could then get to work on; and it seems to me that the United States for the present and for the foreseeable future has the unique responsibility to sort out those problems and take some leadership. Turning specifically to the subject of trade in industrial products, it seems to me that the United States has great difficulty in taking that leadership since it is not entirely certain where it wants to go.

The basis for the current trade negotiations in Geneva, of course, is set forth in the Trade Act of 1974. And the Trade Act has a number of objectives, many of which are in the right direction, leading toward expanding world trade policies and implementing machinery on a more national (economic) basis. This is to be done through the elimination or harmonization of nontariff barriers and through the reduction of tariffs, as well as by the modernization and normalization of procedures that regulate trade. Those are all in the right direction.

On the other hand, the Trade Act has a certain history that led the framers of that act to conclude that probably sticks would do more than carrots to bring about the desired results. Therefore, the Trade Act has a number of measures that one has to characterize as "accentuation of the retaliation possibilities" for those who fail

to agree with what the framers of the law regarded as an improved
international trading system.

Since the passage of the act, it's almost a year now, because
the negotiations have gotten underway with such a slow start, in part
because of a lack of leadership in my opinion, the negative features
of the Trade Act have taken on greater importance than even the
framers of the carrots-and-sticks philosophy had contemplated,
thus presenting a particularly difficult job to overcome. I am, of
course, referring to a number of measures, but primarily to the
utilization of antidumping and countervailing duty procedures, all
of which are being persued in a normal way by the Treasury, I believe,
and by the government in accordance with the law. But, nevertheless,
the law has some features that simply are not fully in accord with
international practice, and certainly not in accord with the objectives
of the act by way of liberalization of trade through reform of the
system on a cooperative basis.

In my view, the Trade Act was framed by people who had a
vision of the United States as a beleaguered giant who needed to
reform the world trading system in order to get a fair break and
that the system was somehow rigged against the United States.
That's why the legislation, when it was sent up to the Hill, carried
the title "Trade Reform Act." The word "reform" was removed
in the Senate Finance Committee, but the idea of reform was, if
anything, given even greater priority. In order to achieve the
reform of the system, the United States' negotiators were provided
with the possibility and congressional sanction of a bag of retaliatory
measures. And in the event we couldn't negotiate successfully, then
at least we had the retaliatory strength in our law to protect our
trade interests against the particular grievances that were most
prominent in the minds of the framers of the legislation—notably
related to subsidization of trade generally and to trade in agriculture
on purely nationalistic and semiprotectionist grounds.

Well, it's obvious to anyone who understood the situation then,
and it's even more obvious now to anyone who looks at the trade
numbers, that the perception of the situation, which brought forth
this kind of trade act, was really incorrect. The decline in the
U.S. traditional trade surplus to a large deficit was not due to the
fact that the world trading system had deteriorated since the end
of the Kennedy Round. Rather, it was due to the fact that the United
States had maintained the wrong exchange rate for an excessively
long period of time. The best proof of that, in my opinion, is that
there has been a shift in the U.S. trade account since 1972 of approximately $32 billion. Now I'm just talking about the surplus. I'll tell
you how I get $32 billion. We were at minus $6 billion in 1972 and
this year we are about plus $10 billion, and we're paying about $16

billion more for oil. Therefore, in three years we have switched, in a positive way, our trade balance by $32 billion without any changes in the international trade regime. No nontariff barriers have been removed, no tariffs have been changed, and no other major conditions affecting trade in industrial products or agricultural products have been negotiated. The economics of the more realistic exchange note for the dollar plus changes in the worldwide business cycle relationships have done the trick—with the help of weather conditions in Russia as a tertiary and relatively minor factor.

In regard to the negotiations presently underway in Geneva, I think that the issues that are present there, with respect to industrial trade, are not difficult to perceive, and the means to deal with them are, I think, rather well understood conceptually by the countries negotiating there. I think what is needed is the will to proceed with some speed.

The main issues as I see them are the lowering of tariffs and getting a handle on the main nontariff barriers (NTBs). It is a misconception in my view to say tariffs are no longer all that important. They are quite important, and especially important in a world that is trying to reduce inflationary pressures. Tariffs have no role to play in the worldwide inflation except to increase inflation and add to costs.

There are certain generic nontariff barriers that we must get at. In general, these generic NTBs are related to government intervention in the economy. I think you begin to get old and dotty when you begin to quote yourself excessively, but I've always enjoyed this statement when I've had more free market talk than I wanted for that particular time to say: "Well, you know there are only two free markets left, the United States and Hong Kong, and since August 15, 1971, we have sort of slipped further behind Hong Kong." Nevertheless, governments are intervening more and more for presumably valid or politically expedient social purposes, and one has to be very optimistic to think this intervention is likely to decline.

In the area of industrial production, the intervention takes place first of all for old-fashioned reasons, namely, to protect old or declining industries. But, more importantly, and this is the focus of my comment from the standpoint of trade negotiations, increasingly government intervention now is with respect to high technology in industries. The Japanese invented that. It's no accident that MITI stands for Ministry of International Trade and Investment.

The Japanese saw the relationship between the fostering of foreign investment in Japan and improving the domestic economy as well as the trade position of a country. Well, the tools by which that intervention takes place are these: government procurement, subsidies (the other side of subsidies, of course, is countervailing duties), and industrial standards. Those three NTBs are the heart of generic nontariff barriers. They are the primary tools of modern industrial policy as practiced in Europe, Japan, and Canada, and they apply to public sector enterprises and increasingly to the private sector.

The subsidies that really count today are not old-fashioned subsidies of $2 per exported beaver skin, but they are low-cost loans for a new tire plant in Nova Scotia or efforts designed to establish a redundant computer industry in Western Europe that could buy its computers cheaply, more cheaply from North America than it could reinvent the wheel, to change my analogy, by creating the new computers from scratch in Europe. And if the individual countries or the Common Market in Europe insist on doing that, then they have to put out research and development grants, and they've got to be prepared to buy the European computers, whether they're good or not, in which case they direct their ministries of posts and telegraphs and their statistical, banking, and other economic organizations to buy the home-grown European computers. And this is industrial policy cum trade policy.

As I said earlier, I do not think this degree of government intervention is going to disappear; it is probably going to intensify.

So the objective in the NTB trade negotiations, in my opinion, relates to the regularization or the establishment of margins that limit the degree of government intervention as it affects trade. Regional policies and other needed social or economic programs are, of course, no less important than trade in sustaining and expanding modern economies. But governments must recognize that they cannot have it both ways—ever expanding liberal trade for the private sector and a sheltered or subsidized public or semipublic sector. I have included in the subsidy category research and development subsidies, and that is complicated because a good part of research and development subsidies, of course, relates to military or semimilitary hardware, and it is not going to be simple to separate that matter out.

To conclude, in regard to the industrial side of the trade negotiations, I have identified as goals lower tariffs and agreements for key NTBs. I would add to that a more rational and rigorously applied international safeguard system, maintained under GATT surveillance.

My assumption is that economic and political pressures will necessitate import measures from time to time by one country or another. And this being the case, the establishment of international standards and a review mechanism will be useful.

I would say, then, that, finally, the question of the developing countries in the industrial products is important and we certainly need something better than the generalized system of preferences (GSP) scheme, because every country that has applied the GSP has some kind of quota or other gimmickry to make sure that the GSP does not really amount to much from an economic standpoint.

Reverting to my earlier point, the essence of the problem, at this moment in trade, is not the organizational one, but the leadership to move ahead. It seems to me that leadership has to come from the United States, and the means for that, in my opinion, is to sort through the problems I have referred to, decide that some of them can be dealt with earlier than others, and set an objective for an early package on one or two of these items.

My fellow panelists in government have heard this from me before. And as I reflect on it, having left the government, I continue to be amazed that I thought so clearly and expressed myself so well when I was in the government. My only regret is that my advice for early action was not followed more assiduously.

COMMENT
Maynard W. Glitman

The previous speakers may have said things that I agree with, but perhaps it is best that I not say that I agree with them. We have fads in international affairs, as in everything else, and in the last few months, the fad is to talk about synchronization. The thesis is that we have got too much of it. For many years, people talked about interdependence and said that it was a wonderful thing. Maybe it is. But we have not figured out a way to really deal with its consequences. Now we have gotten into a situation where we have what I would refer to as hypersynchronization. But the problem is not that national economies have been too closely coordinated; the problem is that coordination has not been effective or appropriate.

Achievement of more effective synchronization would lead to some very fundamental problems of sovereignty, and I don't think there are any international institutions that are capable of dealing with that type of issue. But to the extent that we deal with the sort of phenomena that Harald Malmgren has talked about—increased percentage of trade in gross national product, the closer ties between countries as a result of trade and investment—all of these have tended to link national economies. Yet we do not have a mechanism, other than the systems that were established after the Second World War, to really ensure that we don't get so locked in step that everybody is inflating or deflating at the same time without the balancing of counterforces that existed before the economies were so closely linked.

But, by the same token, the only way that we will ever solve this problem is through the evolution of some sort of international control, and that runs right into the sovereignty issue. So I don't really see any immediate solutions here. I think it's enough for now that we recognize the problem. We will have to work it out from there.

Of all of these areas, I think trade is probably the most difficult one in which to take the large international view. That's in large part because investment or security problems take a little while to filter down to the individual. But in the trade area changes hit the individual right away and right in the pocket book. Thus reactions are very quick and tend to be on a very narrow basis. I'm not saying that as a criticism, it is just a statement of fact. And that makes it more difficult for those of us in the trade field to tell individuals and individual businesses to go ahead and suffer heavy import penetration because it is in the national good.

It also depends on the economic situation. In time of economic well-being, people are more willing to risk reduced protection in return for obtaining lower tariffs in foreign markets. They feel they have more to gain than they have to lose. In situations such as the one we are facing today, the feeling often runs the other way. Therefore, domestic economic difficulties raise a number of problems for trade in general and the timing of negotiations becomes a real problem. That applies particularly to the present round of negotiations.

I agree with both of the previous speakers that the present trade negotiations can deal with the full range of trade problems. Tariffs, nontariff barriers, all of those traditional trade problems are there and the structure of negotiation is such that they can be resolved or at least steps can be taken toward resolving them. Whether or not they are depends upon the degree of political will that is present, and that I think remains to be seen. I think we're prepared to show it, we're moving in that direction; but whether our trading partners are prepared, only time will tell.

The structure of trade with the developing countries is something that I want to touch on a bit. I think Malmgren made a useful point, which I want to emphasize, about the increase in trade from the developing countries. This has been an all too little noticed phenomenon. For example, in 1974, we imported more manufactured products from Taiwan and Mexico than we did from either France or Italy. What this means is that the type of structural changes that the developing countries have been calling for in a rhetorical sense in their repeated demands for a new international economic order are taking place now by evolution based on market forces rather than revolution of the trading system. What we need to do, and what Secretary of State Henry Kissinger tried to do in the UN General Assembly Seventh Special Session speech, is to point this out and to emphasize the need to move from rhetoric to practical developments.

There are really three major issues that are involved in the trade area. One is the question of industrial relocation. It is very sensitive domestically and equally sensitive internationally. I think that we have to face the fact that there are legitimate views on both sides of that issue, but that it is one in which the United States and other developed countries can benefit if we can deal with this issue through a process of evolution that works through market forces.

Another area that has received attention recently is the question of special and differential treatment. This was called for in the Tokyo declaration and it exists already in the form of tariffs through the generalized system of preferences. Special and differential treatment might be worked out in the nontariff area. But to say that developing countries will be given special and differential treatment also suggests that there has to be some sort of a limitation in terms of the duration and degree of such special treatment, and some relationship between that treatment and the stage of development of the developing country. We have to have a process whereby we can do in the trade field what has already been done in other areas, such as in the banking field. We need a system whereby countries gradually assume normal trading responsibilities.

Another problem, mentioned by both Fox and Malmgren, is the escape clause provisions of the Trade Act. I think that we have to recognize that the GSP system, for example, will move some industries from a position of tariff protection overnight to zero tariffs. That sort of thing cannot take place without having remedies available in safeguard clauses. What we may want to take a look at is how to apply these clauses in a more progressive way, including more imaginative use of adjustment assistance. The challenge is to use our existing laws and perhaps develop new policies that allow our own domestic industries to gradually, carefully evolve, with full protection for industry and labor, in a direction that will allow changes to occur without rapid, disequilibrating dislocations either here or abroad.

With regard to the broad institutional framework, I feel very strongly that we want to follow a pattern of evolution and not one of revolution. I think we do need new institutions. I don't agree entirely with Malmgren that we never need any new institutions, that the old ones cover everything.

There are new issues, for example, the environment, that existed previously but nobody thought of or discussed. Thus we need to develop new institutions to deal with problems that haven't been dealt with before and that are not suited for existing institutions. I think we have to be pragmatic about this and not try to overload existing institutions with new issues.

Nevertheless, I think we ought, wherever possible, to try to work with the old institutions, to reform them, to see that they keep up to date. As long as they continue to deal with relevant problems, I think we should try to work within that framework. That certainly applies in my view to GATT. I don't really see much advantage in trying to overturn GATT or include it into some new international trade organization. I think that we have to try to make GATT continually responsive to trade needs. And I think it can be done.

COMMENT
Walter Sedwitz

My remarks will be brief, and I shall stress the problem of the developing countries, particularly the so-called middle-income countries of Latin America. I always feel a bit uneasy when one speaks of interdependence, as if this were a brand new phenomenon. We have always been interdependent in one measure or another. What is new is that the third world has become more articulate and has used political leverage to create greater symmetry in the dialogue with the developed world than ever before. Economic interdependence, therefore, is in large part a reflection of changing international power relationships and economic bargaining positions.

Industrialization and trade in industrial products are still the basic watchwords for the developing countries. It is interesting to note in this connection that the Latin American System for Economic Cooperation (SELA), which was recently established as a new Latin American organization, does not speak about agricultural development and food production as one of the institution's purposes. Rather the stress is on industrialization and commodity trade.

In the 1960s, when the developing countries were much concerned about obtaining trade preferences, their motivation was primarily the result of frustration over the shrinking volume of aid. Therefore, they adopted the slogan "trade and aid." But they found out very quickly, as Harald Malmgren pointed out, that it would take a long time to implement the trade preferences, and that the interests of the developed countries in the trade field were not necessarily compatible with a genuine international development policy. It is clear that the entire issue of trade preferences should have been an integral part of developmental policy and the legislation pertaining to preferences should have been considered by those bodies of Congress dealing with foreign aid.

The fact is that developing country interest in trade preferences has been declining. Partly this is because the larger developing countries, like Brazil, Korea, and Mexico, have been doing fairly well in industrial trade—leaving out for a moment the effects of the world recession. And the smaller countries have been quite frustrated, and justifiably so, with the trade law as it finally emerged from Congress. The bill is, of course, a negotiating device and not a mandate for trade liberalization. But it was understood by the developing countries to open the way immediately for trade liberalization with special treatment for the developing countries, making up for the lack of benefits that accrued to them as a result of the Kennedy Round in the early 1960s.

The upshot is that there is much more interest on the part of the developing countries, especially in Latin America, in an integrated approach to the transfer of real resources. This is a broader concept, encompassing not only trade but also the transfer of financial resources and technology from the developed countries to the developing countries through a variety of new institutions and procedures. It is for that reason that the Joint IMF-IBRD Development Committee was recently established. Thus, in a sense, trade becomes only one aspect of the problem.

In this connection, little has been said so far about the problem of commodity market stabilization. However, it is mentioned in Malmgren's paper. The need for reducing effective tariff levels on processed import products is urgent. In the field of commodity market stabilization, there is ample scope for promoting the transfer of resources for development. I am not convinced that buffer stock schemes, except perhaps for a few commodities, provide the final solution. Buffer stocks tend to even out fluctuations, but obviously cannot reverse any long-term trend. Otherwise the financing needs would be infinite. Moreover, there is the practical matter of how the various existing commodity councils—wheat, tin, sugar, cotton, and so on—might be incorporated or converted into buffer stock mechanisms or agencies.

Perhaps compensatory financing, along the lines of the Lome Convention, offers greater opportunities. The same can be said for the IMF Trust Fund proposal, if it were to cover all developing countries, and not just those with a per capita income of less than $360 per year, as appears to be the intention now.

As to indexation, this presents complex and perhaps even insurmountable technical problems on an international scale, which, in turn, may precipitate political problems. ECLA (Economic Commission for Latin America) is now working on a study of indexation that suggests the selection of appropriate base years or base-year

moving averages for particular products is impossible if the benefits
of the device are to be distributed equitably among the countries of
the Latin American region. The problem is magnified if indexation
is to be applied globally.

As regards the proliferation of new international mechanisms
and institutions for development, this presents a danger. Such
institutional escapism will not in and of itself correct the fundamental
problem of resource transfers to the developing countries. There
is need to work with and improve the institutions, rather than letting
them wither away while new ones are established. It would be far
preferable to make UN-ECOSOC, UNCTAD, and OAS-ECOSOC work
than to circumvent these entities by creating new ones around the
globe.

In this connection, one problem with most existing international
or regional organizations is that they operate with an obsession to
be action-oriented through the adoption of formal resolutions,
declarations, manifestos, codes, and charters. In most cases,
such formal documents, hammered out arduously with all sorts of
escape clauses, do not lead to action. The fact is that international
organizations are no longer, and perhaps should not be, action-
oriented in this sense. Except in a few political fields, maintenance
of peace and human rights, for example, international and regional
organizations should become mechanisms for mutual education,
consultation, and persuasion.

DISCUSSION

Stephen Krasner

I suppose I should address my question to Lawrence Fox. Am
I right in assuming that one aspect of the trade bill requires that
nontariff barriers be submitted to Congress if they are changed?

Lawrence A. Fox

Yes. It is conceivable you might find one nontariff barrier on
which the executive branch has authority to act, but all the important
nontariff barriers require—the agreements require—concurrence by
Congress. There is a simplified procedure so that the agreements
could not be bottled up in the committees. There is an advance
notification procedure, a means to bring Congress in phase for
expedited action. But Congress would indeed have to approve all
of the major nontariff barrier agreements.

Harald B. Malmgren

This is part of the institutional problem in a way, but in the
Trade Act most people have not noticed that what we did was try
to experiment with the congressional-executive relationship in a
novel way. The original proposal of the executive was to use the
veto procedure that has been used under such acts as the Government
Reorganization Acts where the executive can propose a change in
agency structure and then Congress has 90 days to veto the proposal
or else it goes into effect. The Southern senators felt very strongly
as did many other senators, in the Finance Committee and in the
Senate as a whole, that that kind of an idea applied to law in general,
as opposed to organization or defense matters. It could be then
carried over into other matters of legislation and the role of Congress
would be severely impaired. They felt that that was not wise. Moreover, the Constitution does provide explicitly that Congress, not the
executive, regulate foreign commerce. We often forget that, but
the Senate does not. It is an anomaly in foreign policy that in this
particular area there is no power in the executive in the constitu-
tional sense.

The experiment was as follows. To meet the problem of giving
a yes or no answer to trading partners, and not have the issue
frittered away with time, as happened with the American selling
price, it just never came to a vote, never came to action. To
prevent matters of sensitivity from being bottled up in committees
and to prevent amendments to negotiated packages, it was agreed
that the rules of procedure of the House and Senate would be laid
down in the law in advance of their coming up. This is a very novel
thing for the Senate or the House to do. And the issues go to the
House and Senate nearly simultaneously. I will not go into the exact
time frame, but it is almost simultaneous. After 45 working days,
if the matter has not been reported out of committee, it automatically
goes to the floor and becomes pending business of that body, and
must be voted on within 15 days. This makes it hard for a determined
minority to block something. They have to organize a consensus.
And it makes it relatively easier for a veto procedure because you
just have to get one house or the other to be slightly negative. So
in theory this provides a limited time frame.

What lies behind that, though, which is important, is the effort
to tie Congress and the executive into a working relationship. There
are many other provisions of the law providing for consultation, and
consultation with industry and agriculture and labor, so that there
is an interwoven mechanism to prevent a disagreement emerging
later on down the road. It is a very unwieldy system, but it is at
least a try in this area, and it probably could be applied to some
other areas of economic policy. It is an interesting experiment.

In the Georgetown University Law and Policy on International Business article that I wrote with Matt Marx, there is an explanation of this whole procedure and its significance. I think it is the only place it has been written on in public. This might be referred to as a start in that institutional aspect of our international problems.

Seymour Rubin

One of the things that interested me in this general discussion ties in with what went on in earlier discussions. It is the description of a good many of the nontariff barriers as being matters of domestic policy. I recall Edwin Martin's suggestion that one of the problems with respect to agriculture is the fact that you are dealing with domestic policies as much as with international policies. And yet I did not detect in the discussion very much attention to the question of how one really copes with that problem. There was, I think, in Lawrence Fox's statement, if I can attribute it correctly to him, reference to the Michelin case in Canada, where there is the problem of a subsidy, which results from a perfectly legitimate desire on the part of the Canadian government to develop Nova Scotia—a query whether that is that, or whether it is a subsidy, and so forth. Is there any mechanism that can really deal with that kind of problem?

Lawrence A. Fox

That Michelin case, I think, gives the answer. Under this subsidies concept, there could be sufficiently developed guidelines that deal with the problems of regional aids or of starting a new industry. As a matter of fact, some work has been done with respect to regional aids, so that it could be brought under control.

Let me cite an example. This has actually been discussed among some of the officials in the United States government. It is not a government position yet. But, with respect to regional aid, since every country has backward regions, one could establish the following criteria and embody them in an agreement. First, that the amount of the aid would not exceed X percent of the value of the new plant. In general, the European Community follows a 20 percent rule on regional aids. Second, the products would be sold in international trade by the country in approximately historic levels. So it might mean that if we ordinarily get 15 percent of our tires from Canada, if it is roughly in that range, it might be acceptable. If the figure is higher, it could be higher. Third, that the price charged for the products, the price at which they are sold, is more or less normal. It does not look like a dumping price, having had the benefit of a subsidy. Fourth, there could be further clarification as to the degree of subvention. You do not have to charge for the establishment of new infrastructure. If you have got to build a road across a tundra, well that does not make that plant any more productive than a plant that was built in a traditional part of the country that did not have that cost.

I think that the regional aid aspect of subsidies could be dealt with fairly readily. As a matter of fact, in my opinion, it could be broken out of the whole subsidy-countervail problem, because these criteria, if adopted, would be a substitute for an injury test. There would be no need for an injury test, which you know is quite an important issue in Congress.

On the standards issue, we are very far ahead. There really is a draft standards code. It is all procedure. There is no substance there. And if there were the will to go ahead with a standards code in the European Community, that could be wrapped up and presented to Congress, in my opinion, within six months.

Harald Malmgren

I have been asked to explain industrial standards as a category, what standards are, and what the code is about.

The government sets standards for technical specifications, safety standards, health standards, consumer protection standards, standards on what happens to the product after it is used, and the pollution standards after use. Naturally, there will be more and more standards because the public wants standards, and governments are just starting to be active in this area.

The problems arise when the standards are different from country to country, and even more when they are established in procedural ways that create difficulties for people to adjust to. That is to say, if we have an automobile safety standard that is introduced after consultation with the automobile companies in a somewhat surprising way so that there is no time for Daimler-Benz or Volkswagen to adjust for a year or so, they lose the market. That kind of a problem can develop, and of course for developing countries it is even more severe.

So the code, as Lawrence Fox says, deals a lot with procedures. If you want to change standards, there should be public procedures and there should be notification and time for adjustment. And where there are international standards, every effort should be made nationally to work in the direction of those international standards, where certification of end use is a reasonable way to get at the problem. For example, in pharmaceuticals, the French require testing of the process of manufacture rather than what happens to the product after it comes out of the company. That means most pharmaceuticals cannot be shipped into France; the plant has to be

in France so that French inspectors can look at the process. These
kinds of issues are procedural, but they are very important to getting
along with each other and not having standards come up that are at
least in part designed to create trouble for foreign suppliers.

Let me comment on agriculture. We had an experience in the
autumn of last year when various agencies other than the Department
of Agriculture foresaw a tightness in the corn market. Monthly
statistics were evidently showing that there was not enough corn to
go around. This would mean that somewhere in the system there
was going to be a price push upward, which would have a bad effect
on meat prices in due course, and then it would have an effect on
wages and the cost of living indexes and so forth. So by the time
we got to September of last year, it was agreed at the cabinet level
that there should be discussions with other major corn-producing
countries and major consumers to see if the demand were really that
strong, or whether there was a lot of speculation in the market.
We knew we would have export controls if the levels of registered
exports were to be maintained.

Consultations took place and people were sent around to the
various capitals to talk—and it worked. The Japanese government
talked to the traders and asked them to scale back their purchases
to their real requirements. There was an examination of national
requirement estimates in the various departments of agriculture
around the world. There was an effort made with the European
Community to alter the price structure of the community somewhat
to favor wheat, relative to corn, so as to reduce the demand on
corn. And all of this was working quite well until the Russians
came in unexpectedly. You may remember that we had a little
fanfare one weekend about so-called cancellation of a couple of
contracts that we never really cancelled. The process that was
underway then and that continued for two or three months afterward
was one of close cooperation among the major buyers and sellers.
Not to manage the market day to day, not to carry on transactions,
but to prevent disruptive movements in the market and to encourage
a reasonable allocation without any specific formula. And it worked.

In that kind of problem, where you see shortages coming, and
you can usually see them before you get there, government policies
can have an influence on getting through a tight period, particularly
where you do not have reserves sitting around. I think that kind of
experience was very good. It is a pity that it has not been continued.
I think that a regular exchange of views between the ministries of
agriculture in the key countries would do a lot to ease some of the
stresses and strains in grains and in corn as well as in wheat. There
is a certain ideological aversion to it in the Department of Agriculture
because of its basic philosophy that government should stay out of it.

But I think that the rest of us felt that it was a good example of what ought to be done on a regular basis, over and above whatever else we do about conditions of access to markets in the sense of trade negotiations.

PART

V

CONCLUSIONS

9

LIMITED POSSIBILITIES
Stephen Krasner

Expectations of continuous growth and of an ever more liberal international economic system have been shattered by recent events. Western industrial states find themselves in their deepest economic difficulties since the 1930s. The international economic system has been subject to a number of shocks, including the official American abandonment of convertibility in 1971, the imposition of restrictive trade practices by a number of industrial states, the demands of the third world for a new economic order, and the quadrupling of oil prices. Despite these developments, and a general recognition that the postwar system is eroding, the proposals for reform at this colloquium and elsewhere have been modest.

In my view, the absence of radical schemes does not reflect a lack of imagination. On the contrary, it is a manifestation of deep-rooted structural limitations on the possibilities for reforming the international economic system. The postwar economic order was a manifestation of the power and the policies of the United States. That power is now waning, although far from spent. But the domestic consensus on which American policy was built is also weakening. Under these conditions it will be impossible to create a new set of institutions and practices capable of sustaining or augmenting the present, extremely free, flow of goods and factors across international boundaries. Such initiatives would require a powerful state, whose leaders enjoyed broad public support.

Since the beginning of the nineteenth century, there have been two periods during which the international economic system became dramatically more open: the middle of the nineteenth century and the two and a half decades following the Second World War. Both were initiated by states that were economically larger and more technologically advanced than their main trading partners: Britain

and the United States. Both countries played a decisive role in
creating institutional structures that facilitated the relatively free
movement of goods and factors. Britain began lowering its tariffs
in the 1820s. This policy, which culminated with the abolition of
the Corn Laws in 1846, opened the large British market to foreign
products. The Anglo-French Tariff Treaty of 1860 initiated a series
of bilateral agreements that greatly reduced European trade barriers
during the 1860s. The British pound, and the financial institutions
of the City of London, provided the confidence and liquidity that
lubricated the great increase in international trade that took place
during the nineteenth century. Similarly, the United States pressed
for tariff reductions after the Second World War, and the American
dollar and American multinational banks helped to finance increasing
trade. The technological and capital resources of American multinational corporations provided ever larger amounts of raw materials
on a nondiscriminatory basis with relatively few disruptions or
precipitous price increases. The American farm surplus helped
to stabilize international grain markets.

It is not coincidental that successful open international economic
systems have been initiated by states that are relatively large and
technologically advanced. For such states, openness furthers
several collective goals. A liberal system enhances economic welfare, economic growth, and political power. The social instability
that can result from exposure to vacillations in international markets
is mitigated by the relative mobility of factors in advanced economies.
(It is much easier for skilled technicians to move from one enterprise to another than for peasants to plant a new kind of crop or
migrate to urban areas.) Furthermore, a large state has the power
to put an open system into place. It can tempt its potential trading
partners with access to its domestic market. Its currency can
provide a stable medium of exchange. When disparities of military
power are very great, it can even use force to compel other states
to enter an open system. (Such disparities are rarely present today,
but they did exist during the nineteenth century.)

It is much harder to create an open system through negotiation
among states of relatively equal power. Recognition of the benefits
of an open trading system is not enough. The maximization of
global welfare may not correspond with the interests of each individual
state. Today, there are many potential and manifest conflicts. The
United States is much less dependent on raw materials imports than
Europe or Japan; it can afford to take chances that other industrial
states may well find intolerable. The Europeans and Japanese are
more likely to work out special arrangements with their suppliers,
even at the cost of higher prices, than are the Americans. The
governments of the major industrial nations do not order their

economic preferences in precisely the same way. Levels of unemployment that are politically acceptable in the United States would be intolerable in a number of other countries. Britain has been willing to accept a higher level of inflation than other market economies at least in part to avoid putting people out of work. France looks far more favorably on explicit public direction of the economy than does Germany or the United States. Fluctuating exchange rates are more easily managed by large countries with relatively low ratios of trade to aggregate economic activity than by small ones that are heavily involved in the world market. Most states may want an open system, just as most states want to avoid war, but this does not mean that such preferences can be realized.

The differences between advanced and developing states are particularly intractable. While many of the actual demands of the third world have been modest, the immodest rhetoric in which they have been couched is more indicative of the gulf that separates the rich and the poor. The leaders of less developed states are not just interested in intertemporal improvements in the welfare of their populations. They want a basic redistribution of the world's wealth and power. Many want a large slice of the pie regardless of what is happening to its aggregate size. Anticolonialism, a sense of humiliation stemming from past domination, and current failures are the cement that holds the third world together. Symbolic triumphs may prove more important for many third-world political leaders than the modest economic gains that would be secured if the West accepted all demands for reforming the international economic order. The identification of Zionism with racism, which has become a litmus test of symbolic versus mundane politics, has taken place not just in such prominent settings as the United Nations General Assembly but also in more obscure ones like the Food and Agriculture Organization. While there are many states in Africa, Latin America, and Asia with a large stake in the existing international economic order, their priorities are very different from those of the industrial West. It may be comforting for bankers to think of the Saudi Arabian royal family as just another investor trying to maximize return, but this is an illusion that can only produce unpleasant surprises.

In sum, it is very unlikely that states will be able to negotiate a new set of institutional arrangements that could replace the increasingly haphazard structures now governing the international movement of goods and services.

Still, if not strained, the existing institutions may prove quite durable. A liberal trading order does not have to be built from scratch: one is already in place. While it is almost certainly necessary to have a very large and advanced state to establish such a system, it is not necessary to have one to sustain an open system.

The liberality of the last three decades has created pressure groups in virtually all major states with a strong vested interest in maintaining a relatively free flow of goods and services. Multinational corporations are the most obvious example, and their continued prosperity is particularly important for the United States. Intellectually, the experience that still colors perceptions of the international economic system is the 1930s. The lesson learned was that the costs of closure are very high in terms of domestic as well as international economic goals. While this lesson, like most historic analogies, is likely to be proven wrong, it is still a powerful constraint on efforts to adopt policies that would sharply curtail the relatively free movement of goods and services. Despite the decline in America's international power, things may go on without a sharp turn toward protectionism.

One might argue that this analysis is too pessimistic, that there is real hope for the creation of new regime. While the relative size and technological lead of the United States have declined in recent years, it is still the world's largest and most advanced economy. Even at the pinnacle of its power in the nineteenth century, Britain did not possess so much potential power. Why then no hope for the establishment of a new set of institutions under the aegis of vigorous American leadership?

The answer lies in the peculiarities of the international and especially the domestic circumstances of the United States. Internationally, the very size of the American economy reduces incentives to bear the costs of maintaining an open system. America in the 1970s is not Great Britain in the 1880s. Britain was desperately dependent on foreign trade and commerce. The United States is not. American policy makers have less reason to maintain an open economic system than did their British counterparts a century ago.

One example of what might be termed America's relative indifference is offered by recent monetary developments. For more than two decades the United States was a staunch defender of fixed exchange rates based on the gold convertibility of the dollar. This regime was not in the narrow national interest of the United States. For a large state, whose economy is relatively little involved in international trade, it is easier to adjust to external changes with flexible rather than fixed rates: to eliminate a deficit under a fixed rate system a large state has to deflate its entire economy, while with flexible rates, adjustments are made through changes in international prices that have a relatively small impact on the domestic economy. Conversely, a fixed rate system is preferable for small states because flexible rates subject their economy to constant, and sometimes severe, price fluctuations. During the period immediately after the Second World War, the economic position of the United States was so secure that its leaders pressed for a fixed exchange rate system, which made it easier to attract other states into an open regime. However, with the persistence of deficits in the 1960s, American policy makers confronted the alternatives of abandoning a fixed rate system, imposing restraints on the domestic economy, or letting dollars continue to accumulate overseas. They took the first option. Looking beyond the vagaries of American domestic politics and the personalities of the Nixon administration, it was the kind of choice that one would expect a large but declining power to make as the costs of maintaining a liberal international order increased. This is not to say that American policy makers are toying with autarky, but it is to say that they have become less willing to bear the costs of maintaining openness.

Aside from the fact that the very size of the United States makes it less willing to sustain a liberal regime, its internal political structure also makes it unlikely that American policy makers will exercise effective leadership in the future. The American political system is characterized by the fragmentation and decentralization of power. There are many points of access to the decision-making process. It is easy for competing public and private groups to stifle policy initiatives, difficult for central political leaders to formulate and implement coherent programs. In the period following the Second World War, there was extraordinary agreement on the virtues of an open international economic system. The American economy was so robust that even those groups most likely to oppose a liberal regime were relatively quiescent. In the late 1940s, the rest of the industrialized world was recovering from the ravages of the Second World War, and was in no position to compete with American industry. Furthermore, the lesson of the 1930s was that an open international economy would further domestic prosperity, or at least that closure would destroy it.

This exceptional domestic consensus no longer holds. Labor in particular has become disaffected as foreign products have become an increasing threat to some sectors of the domestic economy. Furthermore, as a result of the aftermath of Vietnam the country is drifting into one of its cyclical periods of isolationism. This is most obviously manifest in political affairs, but it can also spill over into the economic arena, particularly when issues concern the developing countries. All of this is not to say that the supporters of a liberal international regime are ineffectual. On the contrary they still probably are more politically powerful than those who would opt for closure (the Burke-Hartke bill was defeated). But it is to say that it will be exceptionally difficult for American policy makers to initiate new policies because of the potential veto that can be exercised by groups that would prefer less involvement with the world economy.

The absence of American leadership is evident in a number of recent developments. After some two years of debate, Congress and the executive branch agreed on an energy bill that is not likely to accomplish any of its major objectives. It is a compromise among competing interest groups, ideologies, and political parties, not a coherent policy. The United States, with more fat than any other industrial state, has the worst record for conserving energy since 1973. The 1974 Trade Bill has elements of both liberality and restrictiveness; while it continues to give the president discretionary power to reduce tariffs (an institutional arrangement begun in 1934 and essential for the tariff liberalization that followed), it also imposes more restrictive procedures for the imposition of counter-vailing duties and requires that the elimination of nontariff barriers be approved by Congress (where protectionist sentiments are more likely to be manifest than in the White House). At the end of 1975, part of the international monetary package worked out by the major industrial states, in particular, France and the United States, appeared to be threatened by the refusal of Congressman Henry S. Reuss and several of his colleagues to accept the International Monetary Fund (IMF) sale of gold to central banks. Reuss's concern reflected policy disagreements, as well as the desire of Congress to reassert itself in foreign affairs. Perhaps the most bizarre recent manifestation of the fragmentation of power and authority in the American polity is the Jackson amendment, which links economic relations with the Soviet Union to emigration policies. Regardless of one's assessment of the merits of this tactic, it is not one that suggests that the United States can carry out a coherent policy.

If leadership does not come from the United States, it cannot come from anyone. No other economy is large enough to take the initiative, or bear the burdens, of creating an even more open inter-national economic system. International organizations cannot substi-tute for the failures of national governments. However, it is possible to take advantage of those institutions that are now in place. The World Bank might become a conduit for capital to develop new sources of raw materials in the third world, as funds from multi-national corporations become increasingly unacceptable for political reasons. IMF may play a more active role. However, it would be foolhardy to expect too much.

International economic liberality will come under attack increas-ingly. Prosperity as well as peace is more likely if the political limits on greater openness are recognized. States should focus their attention on working out acceptable controls on the international movement of goods and factors, rather than on doing away with those impediments that still exist. The United States will have to accept the Common Agricultural Policy of the European Common Market.

America's foreign suppliers will have to accept consumer and environmental legislation and the ensuing nontariff trade barriers. This is not a time for bold new initiatives. Such actions are dangerous, and more likely to be harmful than beneficial. Temporary successes in destroying international economic barriers could easily be followed by dramatic failures if an unexpected catastrophe makes it apparent that there is no state or group of states capable of sustaining the system or of acting as a lender of last resort. For the present, the wisest course is to reform existing structures, not to try to create new ones.

10

INTRODUCTION
Don Wallace, Jr.

We come now to the last session of the colloquium, which is a
round-table discussion without prepared papers. The principal
participants are Seymour Rubin, Sidney Weintraub, and Stephen
Krasner.

Seymour Rubin, executive director and executive vice-president
of the American Society of International Law, is a professor of law
at the American University. He is also an active participant in
international organizations and is currently a member of the Inter-
American Judicial Committee and the American representative to
a new international body, the United Nations Commission on Transnational Corporations.

Sidney Weintraub is an assistant administrator of AID and
chairman of the Inter-agency Development Coordination Committee
within the United States government. Before that, he was a deputy
assistant secretary of state of international finance and development.

Stephen Krasner, formerly associate professor of government
at Harvard University, will be going to the University of California
in Los Angeles to join the Department of Political Science.

STATEMENT
Seymour Rubin

I thought that I might use a bit of your time to talk about the
United Nations Commission on Transnational Corporations. It is
not that I consider that to be the most important organization in what

may be the new panoply of international economic organizations.
Far from it. But it is at least a specific example of what is involved
in this colloquium. It is an organizational response to what is considered to be a troublesome and important issue of economic relations
on the international plane. And perhaps, since we can talk about
this organization in concrete terms, it may help to bring together
some of the threads of the very interesting discussion that has taken
place here.

One thing can be said at the outset about the Transnational
Corporation Commission: the fact that it exists flies in the face of
what would seem to be a common thread in almost all the advice
that has been given here today, which was not to add to the existing
number of UN bodies. Yet here we have another new organization,
adding new luster, if that is the proper term, to the already multi-
faceted jewel of the United Nations. Perhaps the Commission
subtracts something from other parts of that complicated and top-
heavy organizational structure; but it certainly does not simplify.

Another issue arises in addition to that of whether or not a new
organization were really needed to respond to the questions raised
about transnational enterprise. That issue is whether or not this
new Commission can do anything. Can it perform effectively? That
question brings me back to what James Grant was saying a while ago
about problems of agriculture and food—that the problem is really
one of the will of the nations dealing with the issue, and that whether
or not these international organizations work depends on whether
or not such a will exists.

I am sorry to say that I think that that really begs the question.
Some time ago Charles Yost, who used to be the U.S. ambassador
to the UN, made essentially the same argument with respect to the
UN in general. He argued that the problem should not be put in
terms of the failure of the UN, but a failure of the nations that
constitute the UN, and of a deficiency in their will to use the UN
effectively. I don't think that that says anything other than to state
the conclusion. That kind of formulation conceals the strong possibility that the failure of will, the deficiency as seen by those who
want to see the organization work, may exist not accidentally or
willfully but for very valid reasons. At least those reasons—the
increasing extremism of the General Assembly, the inability of its
members to sustain a reasoned debate looking toward reconciliation
and harmonization of views, the multiplicity of members, and others—
may seem to some nations to be a valid rationale for keeping issues
away from the UN.

The UN Commission on Transnational Corporations presents
some of these issues. But at least it exists, despite what may have
been the feeling of some of the so-called home governments of the

transnational enterprises that they might prefer a different, perhaps more expert, perhaps more friendly, forum. One must remember that transnationals hold assets and economic interests abroad that are of substantial interest not merely to the corporations but also to the home governments.

The nature of the problem is at least partially illustrated by considering the membership of the Commission. It is composed of 48 members, states, not experts chosen as individuals, having been decided on as the composition of the Commission. In the membership, one finds more African nations, to take an example, than there are members of the Western European and other groups, which includes the United States, Canada, Australia, and so on. That may be fine from the viewpoint of rectifying the underrepresentation of the developing nations in other organizations with economic clout, organizations like the World Bank and IMF, but it does not seem to me to make for effectiveness so far as the Commission is concerned. If one wants a transference of resources from the developed to the developing, it would seem useful to make sure that the developed nations are fully represented and, since recommendations of the Commission cannot be enforced, in a forum that would make acceptance of those recommendations as likely as possible.

Another issue discussed here in the context of international economic organizations is whether they—new or existing—should attack problems on a global basis. Perhaps other ways of dealing with issues would be better, the regional approach, for example. So far as the Transnational Corporation Commission is concerned, it seems to me that a case could be made for dealing with many issues regionally rather than globally. The problems are, I think, quite different in Africa from those in Latin America because of different degrees of development, different resource availabilities, different trading patterns, and so forth. Even the term "Latin America" is one of dubious merit; there are vast differences in the area, not only of language and size, which suggest that generalization is both difficult and often positively misleading. In any case, it might be better to try some regional approaches, rather than lumping all of the issues of the relations between transnational corporations and the developing nations, from Brazil to the Central African Republic, into one vast category.

Another question for economic organization in general can be drawn from the Commission: Should such an organization, new or existing, try to deal with the entirety of the problem as it is seen or break the problem down into its component parts? For example, should the Commission get into some of the trade-related questions that have been raised about transnational enterprise? As Stefan Robock and Ken Simmonds wrote some time ago, there may be a

"missing dimension" in trade statistics, represented by intraenter-
prise trade, which may not always respond to classic comparative
advantage theory. Should the Commission try to deal with this?
Perhaps a comparable problem is whether or not the Commission
should, in complying with its mandate to put together a "code of
conduct," try for something that is all-inclusive or should it try to
deal with individual issues? Should it, for example, deal with
restrictive business practices, with taxation, with extraterritoriality
under such legislation as antitrust or the Trading with the Enemy
Act, as individual issues, with understandings or standards on each
of these being bound together some time later as part of a more
comprehensive code? I confess to a feeling that if the Commission
takes on the more limited role, developing gradually, it will do a
more effective job than if it aims for the whole thing at the outset.

There is another set of issues illustrated by the Commission,
but that can be generalized to other economic organizations. This
is the matter of how such an organization should operate, as a
rule-making institution or in some other way? In other words,
should the Commission aim mainly at establishing rules or standards
for the conduct of transnational corporations, whether these rules
or standards are overall codes of conduct or standards in somewhat
narrower fields, like restrictive business practices, or are designed
to set criteria for information gathering for general dissemination?
Or should it subordinate this kind of rule making to a coordinative
function, which would give emphasis in the Commission to scrutiny
of national measures and that would aim at harmonization as much
as, or more than, formulation of uniform rules or standards?

The Commission is clearly set on the course of drafting rules
(as well as information gathering and technical assistance). But
there is a great deal of national activity and legislation. For example,
transfer pricing is a matter of concern not only to the developing
nations; the United States Treasury has recently been very active
in this field. There are other areas about which the same could be
said, taxation, for example. Perhaps the Commission could be
more effective as an international organization, and perhaps this
might be a model for other such organizations, were it to give some
attention to possibilities of harmonization, as well as the more
difficult task of establishing accepted international codes.

Beyond that there is the issue of whether or not the Commission
might give attention to a role even more modest than that of acting
as coordinator: that of providing a forum for reasoned and informed
discussion. Again, it might be useful generally to consider the role
of international economic organizations as forums rather than as
action-oriented bodies—places in which experts could get together
on a regular basis to discuss issues with some degree of continuity

and perhaps some agreed on assumptions of fact. One then might expect that the results of such discussions would filter into those levels of government at which decisions are taken, with, one would hope, beneficial results.

Beyond the value of such discussion for policy in the places where policy is really made—the national governments, not the UN— this forum aspect has some merit as being a place in which steam can be let off and perhaps pressures alleviated. In that context, I am reminded of the old suggestion that every government should maintain two embassy buildings in each foreign capital: a regular embassy, in which work would be done, and another sort of embassy, built of very flimsy wood, with light furniture and collapsible windows. The latter would be the one that would be available to be torn down or burnt up whenever there was a riot directed against the nation maintaining the embassy. In that way, the feelings of the mob could be vented in a satisfactory and visible way, but without damaging the capacity of the ambassador and his or her staff to do their work.

STATEMENT
Sidney Weintraub

I shall try to do a certain amount of summarizing and synthesizing of what was said in the other panels, throwing in some personal opinions in the process.

Let me start out with such phrases as "global will" and "political will" and "will of countries," which many have said was the issue in making development relations meaningful. I have been fascinated with such phrases for years. I really do not think that they mean anything. Normally when nobody knows how to make something work, he calls on global will or on political will; or it can mean one other thing, that if the other fellow does not do what you want him to do, he lacks political will.

If global will is an appeal to good intentions, it is meaningless and this really will not work. The issue, I think, is to work out the negotiating techniques, some types of which were cited in several of the discussions today, about how we can really make the international bargains that interrelate domestic and international interests. The need to do this is the essence of negotiating in the fields in which we have been talking. More and more, I think this is at the heart of foreign economic policy.

Edwin Martin raised this issue sharply in the agricultural field; so did Harald Malmgren in dealing with the problem of nontariff barriers and what makes them intractable. In the discussion of commodities, when we got into the question of why there is not a commodity agreement for a particular product, or why commodity policy is so difficult, it is this same issue of the domestic interests differing from international interests. I do not know all the techniques for relating domestic and foreign concerns. I will come to some of these in a little while. But this is the essential issue, not the calling on political will as a measure of good faith. Governments must devise trade-offs and bargains of how to sacrifice some of the domestic aspects of issues in order to gain what may be more beneficial in the international field. There was a lot of discussion on the differences between political forums and specific negotiating forums and specific functional forums. Seymour Rubin raised this issue in his presentation. The political forums need not be just rhetoric, but they clearly are insufficient in themselves.

Let me revert to a question that Lincoln Gordon asked about whether one can get institutional change of a major nature only after a crisis or whether one can bring about significant institutional change in the absence of crisis. My own instinct is that you can bring it about only in a crisis. Crises can be somewhat artificially manufactured, but I do not recommend this as a normal practice.

The Sixth Special Session and the Seventh Special Session were both sort of manufactured special crises. The United Nations Conference on Trade and Development (UNCTAD), which meets periodically every four years, manufactures repetitive crises. We do not change our institutions after these manufactured crises. But there are slow changes in policy that follow from each one of these events. Somebody called these quasievents.

I think one point that Malmgren made is important: The difference between the results following a manufactured crisis and a real crisis is the time dimension. It took 10 to 15 years for the United States to get a preferential tariff system for developing countries that I think will turn out to be meaningless after the manufactured crisis of UNCTAD I. It took a lot less time to set up a world economic structure after the real crisis of World War II. I do not think one year is very much after an event like the World Food Conference to generate too much pessimism on the lack of concrete results, which is a point to which Martin alluded. If a crisis hits us again in the form of world food shortages, then I think we will move fast again. I am sorry that the world is that way, but I think that is the way it is.

One other difference that I would like to touch on is the one between a political forum whose role is that of letting off steam and manufacturing crises, which may lead to incremental changes in policy, and an institution in which we negotiate rights and obligations where there is a quid pro quo involved in the negotiating process.

The United Nations Seventh Special Session and the periodic
UNCTAD conferences, as well as many other institutions that meet
with global participation, result in unilateral demands, and there
really is no end to this process. Some of the demands are justified
and some unjustified, and countries are not likely to respond quickly
to one-sided demands. UNCTAD has some negotiating forums in the
commodity field. The commodity negotiating field tends to be either
reciprocal, as when there is an attempt to balance producer and
consumer interests, or unilaterally demanding, and what it is is
quite crucial to the way U.S. government policy makers will look
at particular institutions. This is the difference between global and
negotiating forums in trying to reach international agreement on
policy measures.

There was a good deal of discussion earlier on incremental
changes in institutions. By incremental change, I think what was
meant was not so much creation of new institutions but rather modification of present institutions. But there is also some incremental
change in the form of creating some new peripheral institutions from
time to time, such as the Commission on Transnational Corporations
or the half dozen or so that Secretary of State Henry Kissinger proposed in his speech at the Seventh Special Session. I share the view
that a good many people here stated, that to try in the present atmosphere to negotiate full-blown new institutions with complicated articles
that have great meaning for countries is probably futile.

The last try at this in an important area was that of the Committee of 20 at which there was some hope that perhaps a monetary
negotiation or monetary system could be negotiated full-blown, with
all the consequential changes this would entail in IMF, and it became
apparent almost as soon as it started that this effort would fail. In
point of fact, the negotiators were always one or two steps behind
the marketplace and eventually had to accept what was happening in
the real world. It is for this reason that I think trying to negotiate
a new international trade organization, whether it is more limited
or more global than the Havana Charter, will not succeed. Let me
mention one or two other examples of incremental versus wholesale
change and then I will state some conclusions.

The group of experts that looked recently at the United Nation's
structure made some sweeping recommendations as to how the
United Nations should be reformed. They recommended giving more
authority to the economic side, increasing the role of ECOSOC
(Economic and Social Council), perhaps eliminating UNCTAD in
time if its role could be taken over by the new organization and the
reformed control authority. It is a good report in the technical
sense. Intellectually, it is a very satisfying report. And yet it is
already being sniped at by developing countries generally and by many

developed countries. My guess is that, when the process is through, there will be very little major change in the United Nations system, but there may be incremental changes. One of the changes that I hope takes place in the UN structure is some change in the way that ECOSOC does its business, by making ECOSOC a more meaningful deliberative body.

The United States, I think, is sometimes considered to be a cynical country when it comes to institutional issues. We have been responsible recently for creating or proposing a whole bunch of new bodies without really thinking through why we were creating them. Let me tell you a brief story. Right after Ambassador Daniel Moynihan delivered his speech at the Seventh Special Session, a representative of a developing country said to me that the standard response of the United States had been that whenever anybody else suggested the creation of a new institution, that there are plenty of good institutions now and why don't you modify them. Then Henry Kissinger suddenly suggested the creation of six or so new institutions. This developing country representative did not necessarily oppose creation of new institutions, but he was commenting on the way we do things.

As I understood what others said—and this is my major point—and what Malmgren argued in discussing institutional issues, it is not so much the institutions, per se, or the creation of new institutions, or even the adaptation of existing institutions, that is important but rather it is the process that takes place as we go through the negotiations or adaptation or incrementation or even the attempt at the creation of a new institution. In other words, despite the fact that no new full-blown IMF emerged, I think that the process of negotiation in the Committee of 20 was an extremely valuable exercise. I think the process of getting the U.S. trade bill through Congress, even though some of its provisions may have been overtaken somewhat by events by the time it got through, was an extremely valuable process. I think that the GATT system of negotiating and also of having a forum for resolving disputes, possibly with sanctions, is extremely valuable. It is this two-way negotiating process that makes GATT, IMF, and IBRD to a certain extent very valuable and the UN somewhat less valuable for concrete accomplishment.

Two final points. There was some reference to overviews, and whether or not we should seek to establish one big institution that could coordinate or oversee all others. I agree with the general view that this is not a good idea. One suggestion was made that the best way to reach agreements was in a smoke-filled room with small groups. This is going to happen in any event, and I do not want to stress that. Whether or not we have institutions, the leading actors in a particular field will get together. They will not always be the major powers: they might be the grain exporters, they might be producers and consumers of particular products.

I do not really think the United Nations General Assembly can be the overview body, which is what the Seventh Special Session has tried to bring about. If ECOSOC were reorganized, and instead of being a mail drop it became a central place where major issues were discussed on a world scale with somewhat less than the full membership of the United Nations present, it could perhaps become that institution. More and more I have come to doubt that even that is possible.

Finally, and briefly since I have little to add to what others have said, I agree that the internal U.S. government processes are not working very well. They are not providing for the kind of give and take and open debate one would like to see in formulation of policy. I agree with what Ray Cline said, that a good part of this is not just the fact that we have bad processes, but that we are not quite sure of what we want in most of these fields.

STATEMENT
Stephen D. Krasner

If I understand correctly, what most people seem to be saying is that we have some very serious problems and that the best that we can hope to do is to take some modest steps to grapple with them. It seems that no one is talking about creating a new international economic order or anything like it. What I would like to try to do in the few minutes that I have is to argue that both the problem and the fact reflect great fundamental structural problems, both at the international level and at the national level, particularly for the United States.

The system in which we are still living, at least the tail end of it, was fundamentally an economic system created by American power and by American policy. It was the kind of system one would expect a hegemonic state to create—a state very large in terms of its economic size, very technologically advanced in terms of the other countries with which it was dealing—and the monetary system it created was institutionally an American system and when it did not work as expected, the people would be basically provided for by the American dollar.

The United States took the lead in negotiating a number of multi-tariff reductions and its participation in those reductions was absolutely critical; raw materials markets have basically been organized in the postwar period by multinational corporations, and most of those corporations have been American, although they acted in a truly multinational sense in terms of ensuring equal access to supply.

And, although I know less about it, it seems also that if one looks at the international food system, it was basically a system that depended upon American surplus and American foreign policy. Food for peace shipments were sent when the United States was very concerned with the developing world and crises created not simply by drought and overpopulation in the third world, but by redirection of American foreign policy toward the Soviet Union and by much increased grain shipments to the Eastern bloc. That system now creates a situation in which the existing institutions are very much in disarray, although that disarray is not yet reflected in actual patterns of behavior. It is not reflected in decreases in the level of investment or the level of trade.

The monetary system (I thought Fred Bergsten's article on foreign policy excellent) is an extremely fragile system in which there is really no overall agreement. It is not clear in the present situation that if there is a crisis of liquidity, who would be a lender of last resort. And that is precisely the kind of problem that precipitated the collapse that led to the depression in the 1930s.

In trading also there are a number of institutional developments that point toward closure. I must say that Lawrence Fox's reading of the trade bill was very interesting; I had read it in a slightly different way, and I could be wrong, but it seemed that one could look at it as a series of measures in which the United States decided it would use more of a stick. It was a situation where, on one hand, one had to recognize a continued commitment of presidential power and authority to reduce tariffs, and, on the other hand, a number of measures having a nontariff barrier submitted to Congress, which proves to be dangerous. It is always risky to have any trade measures submitted to Congress, especially in a situation where there is legal obligation to act on dumping and export subsidies. So it seems that one could regard it as a knife edge and that in the political sense it is a particularly dangerous knife edge that can open the way toward greater closure.

Obviously, there have been bits and pieces of closure in other countries, from deposit requirements in Italy to volunteer automobile negotiations in Britain. One is now in a situation in which, while the system is still functioning, it is much more fragile than it was before. And that is the kind of situation in which some unexpected event—whether it be a New York City default, the malicious use of petrodollars, a drought in the Midwest—could bring this system down in a particularly paralytic way. There is now no one to hold it up as there was in the immediate postwar period and as Britain was able to do in the nineteenth century.

The question, then, is how far can one go in negotiating as opposed to imposing an international order. All of our historic experience suggests that open orders are imposed by hegemonic states. That is not to say that it is only in the interest of those states, but it is to say that the creation of the system comes initially from some sort of dominating state. The real issue now is can we negotiate some kind of new open economic system, or, alternatively, should we try to hand on to the institutions that we have, a much more modest course of action. It does not seem that the former course is the one that is likely to be successful, for I do not believe we can negotiate effectively.

There are dramatic differences among industrial nations. While they all have an interest in maintaining some level of openness, they do have very different interests in terms of their trade dependency, their dependency on raw materials, their national ideologies, their national historic experiences, and, most importantly, the way they approach various kinds of national economic objectives, particularly the trade-off between unemployment and inflation. For instance, there are very dramatic differences in terms of utility function of major states in Germany and Britain. Second, it is going to be very difficult to work out arrangements with developing countries since their primary interest lies in creating a new international economic order through new institutions that facilitate openness. Their basic interest is in getting some kind of real resource transfer. Those are not necessarily the same things.

I now come to the point that seems to be critical to the discussion that we had earlier. We are in a situation that, as Fox said, provokes the leadership of the United States. There is no other place that it can come from. Although the United States is not as dominate as it was 20 years ago, it is still by far the world's leading economic power. The problem is that the United States is a country particularly unable to provide that kind of leadership. Unable, not simply because people are confused or because the structure is temporarily in disarray, but because the structure is almost permanently in disarray. We live in a political system in which the fundamental objectives of the founding fathers, which now seem to be reinforced particularly by the course of history in the twentieth century, were to fragment and divest power to make sure that it was not concentrated in any one place. It did this not only within the government but by giving the press a very privileged status, and though it happened unofficially, by putting a great deal of emphasis on private interest groups.

Even though the United States was clearly the largest power in 1918, it was not until 1934 with the passage of the Reciprocal Trade Act and after the depression and the first World War had taken place that the United States had assumed a leadership role. So, in 1945, when the world was in complete disarray and the American economy was five or six times larger than any other economy, the country finally acted decisively.

In terms of both the difficulty of negotiating at the international level and exercising effective leadership in this government, it does seem that the best that we can hope to do is the kind of thing that was suggested by Lincoln Gordon: we should try and preserve what we have. I do not think we should press forward quickly to try and carry out some of the suggestions Fox made in terms of not trying to do away with government intervention in the market, but try to regularize it and agree upon some kind of general principles. We will have to negotiate greater levels of government interference, not lower levels of interference. There is really no possibility for creating major new international organizations that can somehow do at the supranational level what national states, particularly the United States, are incapable of doing at the national level.

DISCUSSION

Don Wallace, Jr.

I do not propose to summarize. I have heard people say that they agree with everything they have heard and then go on to say something quite different. I am not going to do that. I would just like to pose two questions. Why is this an interesting subject, assuming that it is, and why is it interesting to Americans at this time, or why should it be interesting? It might be that we are simply interested in good management and good planning of world affairs. It might be that those Americans who tend to like order dislike the disorder they see and would like to make things more tidy. I think quite a few people have suggested that. James Grant suggested something different, which really was not picked up all that much— the whole economic system (obviously he was going way beyond political institutions) has broken down. I do not know whether or not that is true but it would be interesting to know how much there is in that sentiment.

Some time ago, Lincoln Gordon wrote a piece in the Washington Post stating that the problem of redistribution was not taking from the rich and giving to the poor, but making the poor richer, which probably is a different problem altogether. I tend to think that he is very right. I also think that Americans underestimate the real problems of redistribution. The problems are not just between the West and the South, but even within the West itself. We are a good deal richer than most European nations, in the sense of per capita

income. I think that the European attitude and position are based
on this awareness, causing almost a resentment on their part. This
places the United States in a peculiar position—many people want
more and want America to have less. From that point of view, my
first question is how important is this set of issues.

My second question pertains to the problem of United States
leadership. Many people today seem to be concerned with this, and
most Americans have become more dubious about the capacity of
American leadership in the world. Even though in the last few
months more Americans have recognized that we should lead, they
feel that it cannot happen. Since I am an optimist, I feel that it has
to happen. The question arises: Could any of these international
economic developments help America in exercising its leadership?
You can say, as Stephen Krasner has said, that we are doomed
because of our separation of powers system. Interestingly enough,
I think that it is reasonably clear that from 1945 until about 1970,
America has exercised extremely effective leadership, notwithstand-
ing this problem. So, I think it can come back. The question is,
how can we get it back? Some say that there are just not enough
bright people around; others say that the government is not organized
properly. I think Ray Cline would say that it is part of the post-
Vietnam malaise. The Economist, in a special issue called "America
in Its Third Century," says that America just may be on a historic
downturn as it suggested Britain was in 1876 (obviously a year
arbitrarily picked). Maybe we are just losing our grip—a lot of
Americans talk this way. I do not think that is true. I think Americans currently tend to be unhistoric, shortsighted, and gloomy.
Could the United States, in a kind of chicken-and-egg operation,
push the world forward in such a way as to enable America to
exercise its leadership more effectively? I think you can say that
some international organizations could have that effect. A good
function of an international organization is to prevent too much back-
sliding in a protectionist direction. Can't we have more of that?
That is my last question.

Willis Armstrong

We have had recalled to our attention by the Wall Street Journal
article of last week on the Conference on International Economic
Cooperation (CIEC)* the rather extraordinary remark of the under-

---

*"Birth Pangs of a New Global Agency," the Wall Street Journal,
October 24, 1975: "The Conference on International Economic
Cooperation (CIEC) is to be the prime forum for dialog between
developed and underdeveloped nations."

secretary of state for economic affairs to the effect that CIEC may be the most significant and most important new international institutional development since the UN was founded. My question is what did he mean or what might have he meant?

Sidney Weintraub

I think I know what he meant. He meant that it would be a terribly important institution. He could have meant it just the other way around.

Edwin M. Martin

I think that this is a very important point. We have a set of functioning UN institutions. We have an industrialized country institution, OECD, which is less and less able to deal with the problems it has dealt with in the past, and we are confronted with this new organization, which has a smaller and somewhat more balanced representation that could make it more effective. It also has competence in the monetary and energy fields, neither of which is within the competence of the UN system.

It seems to me that there are options here that could make a great difference and present very serious problems for the whole international structure. If there are two competing organizations of quite different characters, one divorced from political framework, countries will be trying to pick the organization where their position would most likely be accepted. Chances are that both organizations will be weak. I am rather deeply concerned about the possibility of this developing as a permanent organization rather than trying to accomplish some of the same purposes through strengthening the UN system.

As I was saying earlier, a number of people have talked to me about the need for a study group to determine what new world organization should be established when the UN collapses, which is predicted for some time in the 1980s. Some people have thought the Council on Foreign Relations Project 80 was designed for this purpose. My answer has been that it took a world war to summon the courage to establish the League of Nations and a second war to establish the United Nations. We cannot afford a third one. I do not think that we can put together an organization without this kind of crisis. Therefore, the thing to do is to fill out what we have and improve it the best we can.

I want to make just one other footnote. I believe we are moving into an era in which international cooperation will become increasingly important and institutionalized. I believe this has very great significance for the United States for two reasons. First, the organization of the U.S. government has to deal with foreign diplomacy, with which it has not had very much experience and with which it has not been very successful. The effect of the way diplomatic affairs are conducted bears significantly upon bilateral diplomacy, in the sense that one cannot disregard people who are normally disregarded if they have votes in a multilateral forum.

Second (and this is something the United States can do much about), I think that one of the serious defects of multilateral institutions as they have operated so far is that most countries, particularly the developing countries, are far less equipped than the United States to deal substantively with the issues before the multilateral institutions, either in their capitals or in their delegations. Even where the capitals have competence, they have more important issues in terms of domestic policy and programs than what is happening way off in New York. The result is that most of the time you are dealing with people who are completely free to make up their own minds, but who have no way to get any real knowledge of the substance of the matters and their own countries' interests. Hence, they are easily led by bloc voting or by manipulation of one sort or another.

One of the major efforts that Maurice Strong made with the environment conference and we made with the food conference was to get substantive people in foreign capitals working on the issues. The decision not to leave it to foreign officers or UN delegations was made because most foreign officers are even less well equipped than our own to deal with the rather technical issues that are involved in most of these situations. I have no solution to this problem. It has been proposed that the Carnegie Foundation set up a technical assistance organization to help them. I do not think the United States can play this role. It is a very important problem that we above all must be concerned with if we are going to operate through multinational institutions with wide representation in which our interests will be very much involved with the outcome.

Lincoln Gordon

In addition to the kinds of problems I raised about time dimension and complexity and so forth, I think that Stephen Krasner is right. The system is fragile in the sense that unexpected developments on a very large scale—a food crisis, an unexpected capital crisis—can disturb everything. There are a lot of things that can happen that make crises, but crises do not necessarily lead to good solutions. We may react to crises, but one of the problems in the international economic system is to make sure that countries do not turn inward in a crisis situation. They need to turn outward and talk to each other to find solutions. Right now the system could easily degenerate rather rapidly.

What are the characteristics, in addition to those that I have talked about, that seem to create the problem of leadership in the United States? The first, I would say, is that we are, at least right now, dominated by ideology as to how the system ought to work, without really fully understanding how the market works. My paper on commodities was mainly about the existence of a free market, or what out there is called a free market. When we move away from ideology, we do it with a lurch into extreme pragmatism and set the other things aside.

Second, we are highly departmentalized and this goes back to the traditional differences between political scientists interested in big-power politics and the economists interested in intricate and esoteric matters, such as money and trade. There is, in fact, poor coordination. Instead of coordination, there is bureaucratic competition, which is competition between Congress and the executive branch, competition between USDA and the State Department, competition between agencies.

This leads to a different question, which is style, another head-note I shall make. Our style is secrecy and surprise and going for headlines each day by the person who happens to be in charge of the issue, whether he is secretary of state or the secretary of agriculture. In a complex system such as ours, consensus is required to make a decision. To get consensus, you have to go the opposite route of secrecy. You have to draw everybody in and slowly build a consensus that probably means no headlines, but creating good policy. That is not only domestic, it is international. For example, Henry Kissinger's speech, which is a good step in the right direction, nonetheless does not mention once that Harold Wilson had made a lot of the same noises before. There were a lot of activities around the world in the same direction, and had the speech been in the context of suggestions of others, the reaction in the other capitals would have been more favorable.

Finally, this leads to the question of education. The function of government in education is miserable, if I can say so, in the economic area. Yet we have many studies of what the problems are, for example, the kind of thing that Ray Cline has done. This sort of thing should be done much more, not just by the Herman Kahns or the Ray Clines, who happen to think it is a good idea to look at patterns.

Lawrence Fox

I have only a footnote. I think it is very dangerous to say that we should manufacture a crisis so that we can come out with a good, new solution. Chances are that we might come out with something quite different. There is one way to deal with the subject that is

more susceptible to minimizing the risk. I am not stating this
facetiously. I think in the international economic area there are
at this moment two international organizations that are quite useless:
the UN and UNCTAD. There are probably even more. If you could
say in some appropriate way that UNCTAD will come to an end on
January 1, 1979, unless a new organization is created that takes its
place at less cost with a higher cost-benefit relationship or something like that, this would, in my mind, be a solution. We would
recognize that we are dealing with a self-perpetuating international
bureaucracy that is even less subject to control than the bureau-
cracies in national governments. I am not suggesting that we be
really footloose and say that the UN system should come to an end
by a certain date. That is too dangerous; it might just take place.
We could play a bit with UNCTAD and limit the risks.

David Pollock

It has been a long colloquium, so I will be brief. But I cannot
ignore the last remark, which would imply that this colloquium
ended by endorsing the phasing out—the planned elimination, to be
more blunt—of UN development machinery generally and of UNCTAD
in particular. There is a saying that I would like to leave with
Lawrence Fox: Be careful of what you ask, for it may be given to
you.
    As I said earlier, I'm here really as an interested outsider
and for that reason I spoke only during my panel discussion,
listening the remainder of the time. However, a central question
on my mind throughout the entire colloquium was whether the United
States wishes, as a principal goal of its international policy, to
link the developing and developed worlds together in a more meaningful and mutually beneficial sense—in short, to promote global
economic interdependence. If the United States wishes to do this,
as so many of its official policy statements indicate, then it must
focus deliberately on global economic development. Mr. Kline
has said this, everyone has said it.
    But my point—in contrast to Fox's—is that UNCTAD and other
UN development forums can be as useful for the United States as
for the developing countries. There can be reciprocal benefits.
During the past 25 years, the great powers, West and East alike,
typically viewed the UN as an instrument for their geopolitical
goals. Over the next 25 years, they should view it more and more
as an instrument for the development of all countries, though with
special emphasis for the poorer ones. The UN can be a forum that
would help the United States to do just that: to increase global interdependence without prejudice to national independence.

I believe, for instance, that UNCTAD could be useful to the
United States in this context if the United States wishes it to be.
The United States has often opposed UN policies on development.
This has been particularly évident in UNCTAD since 1968. That is
why Henry Kissinger's speech at the Seventh Special Session could
be such a great breakthrough in terms of a new relationship among
the United States, developing countries, and the UN development
system. It was the moderates, not the radicals in the Group of 77,
who were greatly strengthened by Kissinger's speech. So I suggest
that this process—of aiming at converging benefits between the United
States and the developing world inside the UN—should be strengthened
by your government—not phased out, or eliminated, as Fox suggested.
This was the whole thrust of my talk earlier. It explains why I
believe the United States and UNCTAD can and should be self-
reinforcing, not self-destructing. So Mr. Fox, if you wish this
kind of UN development machinery to wither, it will. But something
else will emerge to take its place—and without your presence.
Remember, if you are not present in new machinery, your influence
in it, as well as the results you get from it, will be weakened. I
can understand irritation with machinery that is not in line with
many aspects of current U.S. policies on development. But if it
is disposed of on January 1979, as Fox recommended, something
else will inexorably come in its place. And it would probably be
far less satisfactory. That is why I said: Be careful of what you
ask; it may be given to you.

ABOUT THE EDITORS AND CONTRIBUTORS

DON WALLACE, JR., a graduate of Yale and Harvard, is professor of law and director of the Institute for International and Foreign Trade Law at Georgetown University. He practiced law in New York from 1957 to 1962, and was deputy assistant general counsel for the Agency for International Development. He was an Eisenhower Exchange Fellow in Europe this past spring, and was on sabbatical as a fellow of St. Antony's College in Oxford in 1973-74. The author of articles and books, including an Introduction to Turkish Law and most recently International Regulation of Multinational Corporations, he is vice-chairman of the international law section of the American Bar Association.

HELGA ESCOBAR, a German citizen, is the assistant director at the Institute for International and Foreign Trade Law. Before joining Georgetown University, she worked for the European Economic Community in Brussels and for the Federation of German Industries. She is a graduate of the universities of Cologne and Munich, where she received her M.A. in economics. Together with the director, she has edited International Control of Investment: The Dusseldorf Conference on International Corporations.

WILLIS C. ARMSTRONG is the consultant for the United States Council of the International Chamber of Commerce. He has pursued a long and distinguished career in the U.S. government and diplomatic service, notably in the embassies in Moscow, Canada, and London (where he served as minister for economic affairs). Formerly assistant secretary of state for economic affairs, he has published numerous professional articles.

C. FRED BERGSTEN is a senior fellow at the Brookings Institution. He has served as a consultant to the Department of Commerce and the Department of Defense and also has held various positions in the Department of State. An author of many books and articles on international economics, he has also contributed to the editorial staff of various publications, such as Worldview, International Organizations, and Foreign Affairs.

HENRY J. COSTANZO is the executive secretary of the Joint Ministerial Committee of the Boards of Governors of the Bank and the Fund on the Transfer of Real Resources to Developing Countries. In the field of international finance and development, he has served in various assignments in Washington and overseas for the U.S. Department of Treasury and agencies administering U.S. foreign assistance programs. During his experience as director of the Office of Latin America at the Treasury Department, he became closely involved in the affairs of the Inter-American Development Bank and later served as its executive director.

LUIS ESCOBAR, a citizen of Chile, is currently deputy executive secretary of the Development Committee. He has been both professor and dean of the Faculty of Economics at the University of Chile and is at present professor at Georgetown University, Department of Economics. In 1961, he became minister of economy, development and reconstruction and left that post to come to the United States as executive director of the International Monetary Fund and the World Bank. He is an expert on Latin American affairs and has written numerous articles and books, including Organization for Economic Development, The Task of the University, and most recently several articles on "Problems of Private Foreign Investment" and "External Development Financing."

LAWRENCE A. FOX is vice-president for international affairs of the National Association of Manufacturers. Formerly he was deputy assistant secretary of commerce for international economic policy. He was a career employee of the Department of Commerce with vast experience in the international trade and economics fields. He was appointed deputy assistant secretary in 1969, having served previously for many years as director of the Bureau of International Commerce.

MAYNARD W. GLITMAN is deputy assistant secretary for international trade policy. He has held the position of economic affairs officer in Canada and the Bahamas. He has also served in the Department of State as the director of the Office of International Trade.

JAMES P. GRANT has been the president and chief executive officer of the Overseas Development Council since its establishment in early 1969. He is also director of various development organizations, including the Pan American Development Foundation, the Institute of Current World Affairs, and the Foreign Policy Association. Throughout his long and distinguished career in worldwide planning and programming, he has published numerous articles on issues affecting U.S. relations with the countries of Asia, Africa, and Latin America.

LINCOLN GORDON is presently a senior fellow at Resources for the Future, Inc. He has taught economics at Harvard University and was president of John Hopkins University in Baltimore. He was minister of economic affairs in London, U.S. ambassador to Brazil, and assistant secretary of state for Inter-American Affairs. The author of several books, including Government and the American Society and New Deal for Latin America, he is also director of the Overseas Development Council.

STEPHEN D. KRASNER is an associate professor in the Department of Political Science at the University of California, Los Angeles. He is the author of several articles dealing with political aspects of international economic relations and is currently working on a study of American raw materials policy.

HARALD B. MALMGREN is at present Professor of Business and Public Administration, George Washington University and Director of Economic Study Hudson Institute. In the capacity as deputy special representative for trade negotiations in the Executive Office of the President, he was chief trade negotiator for the U.S. government. He has authored many articles and monographs on economic policy and international political and economic problems.

EDWIN M. MARTIN is chairman of the Intergovernmental Consultative Group on Food Production and Investment in Developing Countries. He has been appointed to various positions throughout the world, serving as U.S. ambassador to Argentina, economic minister for the U.S. embassy in London, chairman of the Development Assistance Committee of OECD in Paris, and the senior advisor to the secretary and coordinator of the U.S. participation in the World Food Conference.

DAVID H. POLLOCK is the director of the Washington office of the Economic Commission for Latin America. Recent positions include special assistant to the secretary general of UNCTAD and special advisor to the director general of the Latin American Institute for Economic and Social Planning. His work has encompassed operational research and policy assignments concerned with international economic development and with Latin American development in particular.

SEYMOUR J. RUBIN is the executive director and executive vice-president of the American Society of International Law and professor of law at American University. He was with the legal staff of the U.S. government before going into private practice in

1948. He has been general counsel for the Agency for International Development and U.S. representative to the United Nations Commission on International Trade Law. At present, he is the U.S. representative to the United Nations Commission on Transnational Corporations. He is the author of many articles and several books, including Private Foreign Investment: Legal and Economic Realities.

JOHN A. SCHNITTKER, as president of Schnittker Associates, directs the firm's studies in the United States and abroad. When he served as vice-president of Robert R. Nathan Associates, he was engaged in agricultural and food sector studies and also directed work in postal rates, transport regulation, and agricultural trade. He was appointed undersecretary of agriculture and president of the Commodity Credit Corporation. He has written widely on various aspects of the economics of agriculture in technical and popular journals.

WALTER SEDWITZ is consultant to the Inter-American Development Bank. He has served as the executive secretary for economic and social affairs of the Organization of American States. He is also executive secretary of the Inter-American Committee on the Alliance for Progress. He has worked with the United Nations and the U.S. government, and is the author of many publications on economic and Latin American affairs.

SIDNEY WEINTRAUB is the assistant administrator of the U.S. Agency for International Development, also serving as the executive director of the Inter-Agency Development Coordination Committee. He joined the Foreign Service in 1948 and has served in the Malagasy Republic, Mexico, Japan, Thailand, and Chile, where he was counselor of the embassy for Economic Affairs and director of the AID Mission. He has published many articles and essays, including Trade Preferences for Less-Developed Countries: An Analysis of U.S. Policy.

FOREIGN TRADE AND U.S. POLICY: The Case
for Free International Trade*

Leland B. Yeager and David G.
Tuerck

GATT PLUS—A PROPOSAL FOR TRADE REFORM:
With the Text of the General Agreement

Atlantic Council of the United States

THE GATT LEGAL SYSTEM AND WORLD TRADE
DIPLOMACY

Robert E. Hudec

MULTINATIONAL CORPORATIONS AND GOVERN-
MENT: Business-Government Relations in an
International Context

edited by Patrick M. Boarman
and Hans Schollhammer

THE NATION-STATE AND TRANSNATIONAL
CORPORATIONS IN CONFLICT: With Special
Reference to Latin America

edited by Jon P. Gunnemann

THE REGULATION OF MULTINATIONAL
CORPORATIONS

Don Wallace, Jr.

THE WORLD FOOD CONFERENCE AND GLOBAL
PROBLEM SOLVING

Thomas G. Weiss and Robert S.
Jordan

*Also available in paperback as a PSS Student Edition.